Splitting AMERICA

How Today's Politicians, Super PACs and the News Media Mirror High Conflict Divorce

By Bill Eddy and Don Saposnek

Splitting America

Published by High Conflict Institute Press
7701 E. Indian School Rd., Ste. F
Scottsdale, AZ 85251 USA
www.hcipress.com

Second printing: September 2012

HCI Press also publishes books in a variety of electronic formats. Some content that appears in print may not be available in electronic books. For more information on HCI Press products, visit our website at www.hcipress.com

ISBN-13: 978-1-936268-52-8

Library of Congress Control Number: 2012946298

Printed in the United States of America

Cover design by Elle Phillips Design

There are many men of principles in both parties in America, but there is no party of principle

- Alexis de Toqueville

CONTENTS

YOU'RE A CONNIVING, LYING, MANIPULATING NARCISSIST.
AND WHAT SHOULD I DO ABOUT IT, DR. PHIL?
©2006 UNIVERSAL PRESS SYNDICATE

WELL, THERE'S ALWAYS POLITICS...

What's Happening to Us?

Something nasty is happening in America. Have you noticed the trend? There's more bullying, more incivility, more disrespect and even more relationship violence between us at home, at work, in our communities and in the news. And, it seems to be increasing rather than decreasing.

We have noticed a pattern to this behavior that is all too familiar. It includes:

- **Personal Attacks** (calling the other person crazy, stupid, immoral or evil).
- **Crisis Emotions** (which trigger fear and hatred of each other).
- **All-or-Nothing Solutions** (which call for the elimination or exclusion of the "other").

- **Narcissistic Behavior** (acting superior and not caring about anyone else).

- **Negative Advocates** (constantly recruiting others to join in this hostility).

We are well-acquainted with this pattern in high-conflict divorces, and it's not good. This behavior is called "high-conflict" because it increases the conflict, rather than reducing or resolving it. Worst of all, it's contagious – it spreads when people are exposed to it, like a virus.

This behavior results in a state of mind called "splitting" – the psychological term for truly believing that certain people are absolutely all-bad and others are absolutely all-good, with no gray areas in between (Millon, 1996). This might not seem like a serious problem, except for the fact that the spread of splitting leads people to stop speaking to each other, to hate each other and, sometimes, to be violent with each other. It also distracts us from solving real problems. We are now concerned that this behavior is spreading into politics at all levels.

Today's Leaders

Recently, political leaders in both parties appear to be adopting and escalating high-conflict behavior, and perhaps, even leading it. Millionaires and billionaires are funding expensive ads as key elements in high-conflict election campaigns. And, the news promotes high-conflict behavior in every broadcast – to children as well as to adults – by relentlessly showing, and thereby teaching, the most dramatic bad behavior of the day.

We believe that the politicians, donors to Super PACs (Political Action Committees) and the news media don't seem to realize how destructive and self-destructive this escalation of high-conflict behavior can be. We would like to warn them and the rest of the nation about the dead-end nature of this unrestrained behavior that knows no limits.

We have seen splitting destroy too many families, and we don't want to see it destroy the American family. We want to avoid a Democrat-Republican high-conflict divorce. In approaching these problems, it's not about pointing fingers and deciding who is more at fault. It's about everyone taking responsibility for his or her own behavior, and managing collaborative relationships, even when we disagree.

Who Are We, and Why Did We Write This Book?

We are a psychologist and a family law attorney, each who has worked with divorcing families for over 30 years. And, we both are family mediators – we meet with divorcing couples and help them calm down and work together for the sake of their children and their own futures.

We are not politicians or political scientists, but we have learned ways of calming high-conflict families and helping them work together peacefully, for the sake of the children and their parents' future lives.

At a recent conference on high-conflict divorce, we discussed how much the dynamics of the current elections mirror high-conflict divorce. The closer we looked, the more similar these dynamics appeared. In fact, to both of us, the parallels are striking, and the solutions may be too.

We thought it would be worth a try to analyze this and come up with some suggestions for how to change the destructive direction in which we seem to be headed. This book is our small effort to calm this conflict.

How Similar Are High-Conflict Divorce and High-Conflict Politics?

Reports from The Wall Street Journal (Thernstrom, 2003) and from family court judges (Brownstone, 2009) indicate that high-conflict divorce is on the rise. But, some of the most powerful reports come from children who grew up in high-conflict divorce situations and who are now adults. Constance Ahrons (2004) interviewed over one hundred children during the divorce, and 20 years later. The following are typical comments reported:

> Travis, fourteen and the middle child of three, lived with his mother weekdays and spent several weekends a month with his father.
>
>> *It's the old thing – they were playing the kids against each other. You would hear a story from one and then get another story from the other, and you would never know for sure who is closer to the truth than the other. Now, as an adult I have learned to take everything with a grain of salt, and see where it is planted here and there.*
>
> His younger sister also felt caught in the cross fire:
>
>> *It made me really mad. I would have to try to keep my mouth shut to not upset the other. I had to really*

> *watch what I said when I was with either one of them, because - for example, if I would mention my father while I was with my mother, that would really set her off.*

> Unfortunately this resulted in her distancing herself from both parents. "I don't remember ever having this feeling like, oh, I can't wait to see my dad or mom now. I really miss them! Instead, it was always a relief to get away from the other" (p. 80).

Did you notice how the children were turned off to both parents, because of their high-conflict behavior? But of course, politicians wouldn't act this way, would they?

More recently, it seems that they are acting in very similar ways:

> On the first floor of the Capitol, there is a private dining room for senators, the "inner sanctum," where Republicans and Democrats used to have lunch (at separate tables, but in the same room). In the seventies, old bulls such as James Eastland, Hubert Humphrey, and Jacob Javits held court there; later, Daniel Patrick Moynihan did. "You learned, and also you found out what was going on," Dodd said, adding, "It's awfully difficult to say crappy things about someone that you just had lunch with."

> These days, the inner sanctum is nearly always empty. Senators eat lunch in their respective caucus rooms with members of their party, or else "downtown," which means asking donors for money over steak and potatoes at the Monocle or Charlie Palmer. The tradition of the "caucus

> lunch" was instituted by Republicans in the fifties, when they lost their majority; Democrats, after losing theirs in 1980, followed suit. Caucus lunches work members on both sides into a state of pep-rally fervor. During one recent Republican lunch, Jim Bunning referred to Harry Reid as an idiot. "At least he had the courtesy to do it behind closed doors," Alexander joked, adding, "We spend most of our time in team meetings deciding what we're going to do to each other."
>
> In 2007, Alexander and Lieberman started a series of bipartisan Tuesday breakfasts. "They kind of dwindled off during the health-care debate," Alexander said. Udall has tried to revive the Wednesday inner-sanctum lunch. For the first few months, only Democrats attended. Then, one Wednesday in May, Susan Collins, the Maine Republican, showed up, joking nervously about being a turncoat; to protect her reputation, her presence was kept secret.
>
> These efforts at resurrecting dead customs are as self-conscious and, probably, as doomed as the get-togethers of lovers who try to stay friends after a breakup. Ira Shapiro, a Washington lawyer and a former aide to Senator Gaylord Nelson, of Wisconsin, put it this way: "Why would they want to have lunch together when they hate each other?" (Packer, 2010).

Who's in charge here when children, and Senators, feel that they have to keep secrets to protect themselves from their high-conflict families? And, as the boy above said: "You would never know for sure who is closer to the truth than the other." Doesn't this fit many of today's politicians?

Endless Polarization

It used to be that politicians said whatever it took to get elected. Then, after the elections were over, they became reasonable and worked together for the good of the nation. Today, we are seeing splitting continue after the election, in our 24/7 news cycle.

As a result of this continued polarization, some of the reasonable politicians – the people who could work together – are no longer trying to stay in office, but are divorcing themselves from their professional partners.

> Olympia Snowe, Maine's retiring US senator, announced Friday that her reelection campaign committee has transferred $1.2 million of its remaining funds to an effort to encourage young women to participate in public service. **Snowe, who cited partisan polarization in her decision earlier this year not to seek reelection**, said the money will go to the Maine Community Foundation to support the Olympia Snowe Women's Leadership Institute. Snowe, a Republican, will establish that institute after she completes her third term in the Senate. Of the remaining balance, about $800,000 is being used for outstanding campaign obligations and to establish a multicandidate committee whose goals are to diminish what Snowe sees as polarization in today's political environment. (AP)
>
> From the Boston Globe, July 14, 2012 (bold added)

With reasonable people dropping out of politics, will high-conflict politicians be all that remain?

About this Book

The next two chapters focus on what we have learned about the key dynamics of high-conflict divorce – from those of the Fiery Foes to the negative advocates, to the splitting dynamic, and more. Then, the following four chapters examine how politicians, Super PACs and the news are increasingly appearing just like high-conflict parents – with the same alienating effect it is having on voters as on the children.

The last chapter looks at how we might heal, rather than split, our nation. As a little extra, we included a High-Conflict Politician Scorecard in the Appendix. You can use it to analyze your favorite leaders and decide for yourself.

We hope you take this book seriously – but also enjoy the humor, to make sense of the nonsense of those personalities we discuss who seem intent on splitting our American family.

"Well, if it doesn't matter who's right and who's wrong, why don't I be right and you be wrong?"

Chapter

2

How Did Divorce Get So Ugly?

The Individual Versus the Family

When times were simpler, we had to work together to get most things done. There was a sense of cooperation most of the time with the people close to us. The group was more important than the individual. Our goals were shared and long-term plans tied us together. We knew we were connected and needed to get along to survive and thrive.

As family structures and society have grown more complex, it's harder to see and appreciate the bigger picture of our common goals. We seem to have gone the other direction, as we oversimplify, dismiss, and label negatively anything that's complex. Now, the leaders who are responsible for dealing with complex problems are blamed for these problems and for not "making things work better." In families, couples increasingly turn their frustrations on each other, and in politics, politicians increasingly blame each other for all that is wrong. This trend has continued to the point at which relationships in marriage, family, and country all appear to be in peril. However, it is important to make some distinctions regarding how people respond to these changes. In this chapter, we will look at the situation of divorce, and in the rest of the chapters, we will show how the family in divorce (in its high-conflict state) is mirrored by today's politicians.

Four Types of Divorcing Families

A well-known divorce researcher, Constance Ahrons, has identified five different types of parental relationships that develop after a divorce: Perfect Pals; Cooperative Colleagues; Angry Associates; Fiery Foes and Dissolved Duos (Ahrons, 1994; 2004). They are listed below and described in order from least amount of relationship conflict to most conflict. Dissolved Duos is a category of divorced families in which, after the divorce, one parent leaves the area and detaches completely from the previous family, so we will leave that category out of our discussion.

PERFECT PALS are parents who were best friends during the marriage and remain best friends during and after the divorce. They dissolve their legal marriage and part amicably, using self-help books or simple consultations with an attorney, if even needed. They continue to share their children frequently and supportively, attend their child's school and extracurricular events together and sit together, and they share holidays and vacations together (even together with their new spouses). Their children are among the most well-supported – financially, emotionally, and socially – of any children of divorce.

Cooperative Colleagues are parents who do not like each other as people but remain committed to supporting and respecting each other as parents to their children. They dissolve their legal marriage using mediators or separate attorneys, and often consult with mental health professionals for assistance in developing a Parenting Plan (i.e. custody and visitation plan). Occasionally, they may use litigation to resolve more difficult financial issues. They share their children with mild to moderate degrees of conflict, attending their children's school and extracurricular events together, but sit separately. They celebrate separate holidays, birthdays and vacations, and mostly have minimal contact with each other.

Angry Associates are parents who do not like each other as people and do not respect each other as parents. They dissolve their marriage using separate attorneys, mostly in litigation. They do not share their children without a fight over most every detail. They regularly sabotage each other's parenting time, bad-mouth each other to the children, argue and litigate over financial support issues repeatedly, and frequently have bitter and tension-filled transfers of the children. When attempting to talk on the phone with each other, they often call each other names and frequently hang-up on one another…all in ear-shot of the children. They maintain separate universes of celebrations with the children, and if they show up at the same school event, there are glares at each other, dismissals of the other's presence, and guilt-tripping of the children for greeting the "other" parent first after a soccer match.

Fiery Foes have been called the "Inveterate Litigators" and the "Holy Warriors of High-Conflict." They are parents who despise each other and deny any importance of the other as a parent to the child. In fact, they most often see the "other" parent as a destructive force on the children, and they bad-mouth each other regularly to the children and to anyone else who will listen. They regularly take each other to court for any number of minor issues, spending tens of thousands of dollars on attorney and court fees each year. They regularly have restraining orders on each other, slander each other publicly whenever given the opportunity, and often withhold or even abduct the children from each other. They regularly accuse each other of the most heinous acts, including child molestation, physical abuse, domestic violence, stealing money, threats of homicide, parental alienation, sabotaging services for their child, poisoning the well among extended family, friends, teachers, doctors, therapists, lawyers, and, of course, judges.

The children of these "Fiery Foes" frequently develop symptoms of PTSD (post-traumatic stress disorder), similar to children living in a war-zone. They are hypervigilant, anxious, depressed, suicidal, aggressive, substance-abusers, school drop-outs, and, if put in the hands of a diagnostician, will come away with labels such as ADHD, Bi-Polar, Conduct Disorders, Depression, Anxiety Disorder, and more. They will often be put on strong medications, as a result. All of this happens while in the care of professionals who may not even know of the difficult divorce through which these children have been living.

High-conflict divorce requires only one party to start it, but two parties to play it out.

When we talk about high-conflict divorce, it usually refers to the Fiery Foes, but also to the Angry Associates. For some years after the divorce, approximately 60% of couples remain in significant conflict with each other. But, by 10 years after the divorce, 18% have become "Dissolved Duos", and 22% remain "Angry Associates" or "Fiery Foes" (Ahrons, 2004). For those 22% of divorcing couples, the conflict never ends. Ironically, those same kinds of high-conflict dynamics are rampant in contemporary politics.

After we lay out the fundamental ways that high-conflict divorce works, we will show you how these dynamics play out in Congressional and Presidential elections.

High-conflict divorce requires only one party to start it, but two parties to play it out. And, as we will discuss in the next chapter, this high-conflict "game" is contagious and sucks innocent people around it into the middle of the dynamic.

Tribal Warfare

Divorce researcher Janet Johnston describes an interesting characteristic of high-conflict divorce. She calls it "Tribal Warfare" because of its close similarity to the way that many primitive tribes deal with their conflicts (Johnston & Campbell, 1988). It's defined as the gathering of friends, family, and professionals into "sides" for the child custody "battle" to launch and sustain.

Once the dispute begins (generated by either one or both parties), the "tribes" join in the fight as supporters of their respective sides and keep the fight going. As long as both participants and their tribes continue to threaten each other in back and forth acts of mud-slinging, the custody fight goes on and on and on.

Who's Responsible for the Fight?

We used to think of child custody fights in family court as always started and maintained by both parents equally.

Now we know that there are at least three kinds of high-conflict divorces:

1. **One High-Conflict Person (HCP)**
One of the parties regularly engages in high-conflict behavior in many parts of his or her life – this behavior is part of his or her personality. The other person is a reasonable person and rarely (or never) engages in high-conflict behavior. The HCP, or "conflict host" (a term described by Rutgers psychologist, Ken Kressel), manifests high-conflict behavior and continually provokes the other party (who does not want conflict but is driven by the conflict host to defend him or herself against the blaming and accusations). The reasonable person starts to "mirror" the same behavior of the high-conflict person. By the time they reach a divorce professional, they are both embroiled in the battle – and it often looks like two HCPs fighting, even though it isn't.

2. **Two High-Conflict People (HCPs)**
Both parents regularly display high-conflict behavior with each other and with others and mutually provoke each other until a pattern of high-conflict behavior is established and sustained. They both have high-conflict personalities.

3. **High-Conflict Environment**
Neither parent regularly displays high-conflict behavior in their lives. Neither has a high-conflict personality. But once they get involved with the family court system and tribes of attorneys, other professionals and advice-givers (family, friends, co-

> workers and so forth), they are induced to behave like adversaries and succumb to the larger system that encourages and maintains high-conflict behavior.

We have learned from all this that it takes two people to fight, and only one to not fight.

We feel that ultimately everyone who engages in high-conflict behavior is responsible for this problem. We have learned from all this that it takes two people to fight, and only one to not fight. However, because the dynamics of conflict are so powerful, it is very difficult for most to resist a conflict "host's" invitation to fight. Moreover, the system that we use for divorce (and politics!) encourages this dynamic (more on this point later).

Re-Writing History

Divorce researcher Janet Johnston also describes another interesting phenomenon that happens in high-conflict divorces. Each parent, over time, begins to see the other as a villain. They attribute negative characteristics to the other in such extreme ways that they actually re-write marital history and everything they knew about their partner to appear completely negative (Johnston & Campbell, 1988). This is an example of splitting. Since the other person now is "all-bad", they come to believe that anything good in the past couldn't have really happened.

By cherry-picking only negative examples (and having it fueled by the "tribe"), they reconstruct the identity of their spouse into a caricature of an evil, horrible person. So, for example, a man who was once considered to be a loving husband and father is now re-characterized by the wife as a violent, angry, abusive man, who the children are now afraid of... and who may even be a serial killer!

A woman who was once the love of her husband's life and the best mother in the world now is re-characterized by him as a detached, unloving, manipulating, money-grabbing person, who never wanted children, never loved the children, and certainly never loved him! She is turning the children against their father and, therefore, she should have only minimal contact with the children.

These re-written histories are based upon fear, resulting from decreased contact that the parents have with each other once the divorce process begins. The adversarial family court system for divorcing couples (including the attorneys, the courts, and even their family and friends) encourages them to shift from being partners to becoming enemy combatants. The power of this dynamic is like a tornado...sucking in everyone around the conflict and twisting reality until it and the people involved are unrecognizable.

The spouses become reconstructed as exaggerated, cartoon-like caricatures of themselves. In court, these caricatures are presented as the attorney's "briefs" on the case; each side making the other side look as horrible as possible, in attempts to "win" the battle. However, when one parent "wins" in family court, everyone loses, especially the children.

Relationship Conflicts

Many conflicts are those with two parties in dispute over some clear and single issue, like a minor car accident, in which one person rear-ends the other and causes damage to the car. Once the parties settle the amount that it costs to repair the vehicle, the dispute is over, and the parties will likely never meet again. However, relationship conflicts involve many aspects to the disputes, like those in divorce and politics; they have multiple levels contributing to them. The parties are in a longer-term relationship with one another and must figure out how to settle their disputes in a way that maintains their on-going relationship.

Such relationship conflicts arise in divorces involving children, in which the parents will continue to be co-parents of the children forever, and, as such, will need to have on-going contact with one another for years to come. They must try to resolve their conflicts about many issues that arise during the divorce and the many issues that come up for years after the divorce, such as child and spousal support and time-sharing of the children. Ideally, they will resolve these disputes in ways that minimize damage to their children. Similarly, politicians must work together with each other as cooperatively as they can to try to resolve their differences over the many issues that they work on daily. Sometimes, however, the parties cannot agree and become "stuck" and unable to resolve their differences.

Reasons Divorcing People Get "Stuck"

There are several major reasons why spouses in conflicts during divorce get "stuck" and cannot resolve their conflicts:

1. **Personal reasons**, as when one person in the dispute has a personality problem which makes that person a "high-conflict person" (HCP) or "conflict host." Even in the face of a reasonable person on the other side, the person will simply not allow a resolution to the conflict, and sabotages every reasonable effort to reach agreement.

2. **Interpersonal reasons**, such as when there is an ongoing negative relationship between the parties (bad chemistry), and each person regularly sabotages any positive idea offered by the other person – they get stuck in an endless loop of fighting, no matter what they talk about. These high-conflict couples in divorce, and in politics, can play out this drama for years.

3. **Tribal reasons**, as in the idea of "tribal warfare" described above, in which friends, family, attorneys, therapists, and the court system itself keep the parties in the fight by continually fueling the flames, as the many players in the two-party adversarial political system also do.

4. **Legitimate differences in points of view**, in which two reasonable parties have different points of view that are very difficult to reconcile. For example, one parent may think that private school would give the best education to their son, while the other parent believes that public school would be best.

Hidden Agendas in Divorce

People are way more complex than they appear. For example, in divorce, one spouse might ask for full custody of her child, claiming that she is the better parent, whereas what she really wants is to increase her child support so that she can survive financially. Or, another spouse may insist on joint custody, claiming that all the research shows that children need both of the parents equally, whereas what he really wants is to regularly come over to his estranged spouse's house during the frequent transfers of the child in hopes that he might be able to persuade her back into the marriage with him.

Another possibility is that a spouse may insist on 51% of custody with a child with whom he or she rarely spent time during the marriage. Sometimes, what that spouse really wants is to assert power (having 1% more) over the other spouse who left the marriage. It is very common for spouses in dispute to have such hidden agendas as their real motives in requesting certain outcomes of custody fights (Saposnek, 1983; 1998). Certainly, in politics, hidden agendas are rampant, complex, and often convoluted.

Parental Alienation of a Child

Probably the cases of custody battles with the highest levels of conflict are those involving "Parental Alienation Syndrome," more recently termed "The Alienated Child" (Kelly & Johnston, 2001). In these cases, a child puts down the other parent and refuses to have any contact and resists all visitation and communication with that parent. The child can give no clear or valid justification for refusing contact with the parent. Presumably, the favored parent contributes to alienating the child against the other parent by vili-

fying the target parent and joining with the child (sometimes very subtly) against that parent.

The child will take very drastic measures to avoid that parent at all costs, including threatening or even attempting suicide if forced to be with that parent. While this extreme behavior has many complex dynamics beyond the favored parent's input, it illustrates the complete irrationality that can result within a very high-conflict divorce – irrationality that can be deadly to a child caught in the middle of it.

These types of cases are very intractable and resist treatment. Over time, the negativity in the cases escalates, with compounding charges of child molestation, physical abuse, and parental neglect leveled against the alienated parent – mostly based upon no credible evidence. The all-bad thinking may largely be a result of the child absorbing a parent's splitting state of mind. This is compelling evidence of a truly "split" family that resists repair.

Negative Advocates

High-conflict divorces are heavily influenced by "Negative Advocates." These are members of the parent's "tribe" – family members, friends and/or professionals – who aggressively advocate for a high-conflict person's negative emotions, negative thinking and negative behavior. Most high-conflict cases have at least one high-conflict person and at least one negative advocate. It's hard for either of us to remember a high-conflict divorce case that didn't involve one or more negative advocates.

Negative advocates appear emotionally hooked and uninformed. They can be anyone who gets close to an HCP and absorbs their negative emotions, thinking and behavior. They start to mirror that behavior and may even become more aggressive than the HCP. One example is how often family members fund their relatives' child custody battles. They often develop an extreme dislike or hatred for the other parent of the child. This may have begun well before the parents split up, or after the divorce proceedings began. In either case, any positive feelings turn completely negative in their attitude towards and their own interactions with the other parent during their interactions with the child.

A Team of Negative Advocates

We have each seen cases in which a whole team of family members showed up to say awful things about the child's other parent. In one very high-conflict custody case, the losing parent's family was in the audience and started booing the judge who made the decision. They were quickly ushered out of the courtroom by the bailiff. This was certainly a great example of tribal warfare at its finest. In some cases, negative advocates themselves are high-conflict people, which was the case in this example. But, in the majority of high-conflict cases, the negative advocates appear to be ordinary people who become emotionally hooked by an HCP, but are simply uninformed. Then, they start mirroring the high-conflict person's statements, emotions and behavior.

Often, once they become informed as the case progresses, negative advocates stop supporting the HCP. In many cases, we have seen friends, neighbors and co-workers become heatedly involved in a person's divorce, then suddenly drop out of the case and disappear as friends, after they were exposed to more information – especially when they learn about the history of their friend's own high-conflict behavior!

Professionals as Negative Advocates

While negative advocates can be anyone in any dispute, especially one with an HCP involved, some of the most difficult and powerful negative advocates are the professionals who escalate the conflict – purposely or inadvertently. They generally hurt their HCP clients by justifying their bad behavior so that it doesn't change, or it even gets worse. They are just like the "enablers" of an alcoholic or addict, who help the person stay addicted by encouraging the negative behavior related to their use of alcohol or other drugs.

One example that may surprise you is when therapists become negative advocates. Because they often work only with one of the parties in a divorce, their influence imbalances the delicate dynamic between the couple. Moreover, because they connect on an emotional level with their client, they feel close to and protective of their client and, as a result, they unwittingly often wind up siding with that client against the other spouse and often refuse to see or have any contact with the other spouse, even when requested. This simply fuels the mistrust and anger of the other spouse, and actually increases the level of conflict between the divorcing spouses. The therapist has now solidly become a negative advocate for his or her client!

Another, more expected example is found in every family court system. There are a few lawyers who have a reputation for being high-conflict litigators. They are often highly paid. Some of them are HCPs themselves. This is just part of who they are, and they repeatedly engage in high-conflict behaviors. This is destructive to families, but they are well paid to do so by their HCP clients. While some people would complain that the whole family court system of professionals is damaging and unethical, this appears to be a minority of perhaps 10% of lawyers and other professionals. Yet even 10% is substantial and they keep many cases escalated into high-conflict behavior unnecessarily. The following is an example of this dynamic:

A Hollywood Example

Let's reflect on a Hollywood divorce. Kim and Alec are award-winning actors on television and the big screen. For approximately ten years, their high-conflict divorce played out in family court – and in the national news. It had all the dynamics of concern to us. Since most high-conflict families don't make the news, we'll use this as an example, because it has been written about so much and it contained many of the common dynamics that increase, rather than decrease the conflict.

Each parent claimed to have their daughter's best interests at heart. Kim, in extreme and unsupported terms, accused Alec of being a violent brute. Alec, in extreme and unsupported terms, accused Kim of alienating their daughter. Ultimately, you might wonder how it could be in their daughter's best interest for each of her parents to claim that the other parent was one of the worst parents to ever walk the earth.

In the process, they would gather many people around them who seemed like negative advocates. Kim's advocates would say that he was an aggressive and dangerous man. Alec's advocates would say that she was alienating their daughter against him and ruining her childhood. Maybe one of them was right – or maybe both were right. The reality in family court is that it's very hard to get a clear perspective to these complaints, since they are largely based on "he said, she said" information.

In the middle of the tug of war, Alec left an angry voicemail message for their daughter when she didn't answer his scheduled phone call. Then, "someone" (reportedly a negative advocate for Kim) released the voicemail message to the media, and the negative advocates lined up on both sides, proclaiming throughout the news media the culpability of the other side:

Kim's advocates said it was all his fault: "See, this voicemail proves what a brute he is!"

Alec's advocates said it was all her fault: "See what she drove him to! You would do the same thing if you had to deal with Kim and her endless alienation of your daughter against you." As illustrated, negative advocates tend to get over-involved and make things worse.

Then, when Alec and Kim were back in court, after their daughter allegedly refused to see Alec, and after he had sent her an apology letter, the following took place. See if, in your opinion, this scene has any negative advocates:

> *During the proceeding in June, [my ex-wife's lawyer] brandished a letter of apology that I had sent to my daughter and plopped it in front of me in the witness box. The letter had been torn in half, presumably by my daughter. In order to put his signature touch on this, [the lawyer] bent over to arrange the severed pieces to form a recognizable whole. Right to the end, [the lawyer], one of the most malicious human beings I have ever encountered, never missed an opportunity to 'advocate' on behalf of the truly angry litigant. Their goal was to show that my daughter did not want to see me again. More than $3 million in*

> *joint legal fees had been spent. In my mind, all of it was a buildup to this; so that [the lawyer] and his client could have the pleasure of sticking that letter in my face (Baldwin 2008, p. 185).*

The judge resolved this issue – and put the brakes on their high-conflict behavior – by telling them to stop commenting in public, or there would be severe consequences. Eventually, the judge also ordered substantial contact with each parent, so that the tug of war over their daughter could end. While both parents may have some deficits, neither parent has turned out to be the evil monster that the other described in court for several years.

Blatantly False Statements

One of the sad realities of high-conflict divorce is that negative advocates can make false statements and get away with it. Complaints about this have significantly increased over the past ten years, but there seems to be little that can be done about it – much the same as in today's politics.

In family courts, making false statements under "penalty of perjury" is a crime. However, family courts are civil courts, not criminal courts. This generally means that to prosecute the act of lying under penalty of perjury would take action by the district attorney, which is not exactly a priority in any court system. In California, a search of prosecutions for lying under penalty of perjury produced only one appellate court case and the punishment in that case was probation. Thus, the usual "penalty" in high-conflict divorce cases is that the person who is lying is more likely to be found less credible than the other party and may lose the hearing – but not the war. So it keeps on going and going.

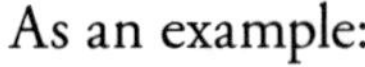

As an example:

> In an early hearing in a case, the attorney for the wife said that the husband was "coming around the house and frightening her." This turned out to be a blatantly false statement, as the wife had written in her declaration that he was, in fact, staying away from the house and that she was not seeking a restraining order. This was a woman who had requested and received a restraining order against her husband a year or two earlier, based on false allegations about him assaulting her – when, in fact, he was out of the state and was able to prove that to the court. But, after her lawyer said that her husband was "coming around the house," the judge looked with a frown at the husband. His lawyer asked to respond, but the judge said there wasn't time. "Since she is not seeking a restraining order," the judge (who wasn't involved the prior year) simply said: "Mr. Smith, I'm admonishing you to stay away from her and the residence."

The damage was done, and this false assertion influenced the judge throughout the rest of the case. The stereotype of the husband as an aggressor was set in place. There was no time to correct the false impression. Her negative advocate got his comments in and then got out without an opportunity for accurate information to be considered.

"It's a full-bodied wine with hints of acrimony, partisanship, and moral outrage."

Chapter
3

How "Splitting" Generates Hatred

In high-conflict divorce, children often grow to hate one of their parents – even a parent they were very close to and loved just a year or two earlier. It's an intense hatred and disdain that is deeply emotional. They can think of nothing good about that parent (the "rejected" parent), and they can think of nothing bad about their favored parent. It's an example of how high-conflict behavior creates splitting in the minds of bystanders – in this case, the children. How does this happen?

Many high-conflict divorces are driven by one or two parents with borderline or narcissistic personality disorder (Eddy & Kreger, 2011). One of the traits of this disorder is "splitting" people into those who are all-good and those who are all-bad, in their minds. Sometimes they even see themselves as all-good one day and all-bad the next. You might think that's weird and decide to avoid such people. But you can't – there are too many of them.

Splitting is unconscious and contagious – just like the effects of advertising. It gets past your radar and you come to believe it – unless you realize what is happening. The reason is that high-conflict emotions are highly contagious. If you're in a high-conflict emotional environment, you will "catch" this splitting tendency and start to view people as all-good or all-bad, as well. Children are especially vulnerable to absorbing splitting, but adults do as well – especially in high-conflict divorce and, as we are now observing, in high-conflict politics.

For example, in high-conflict divorce, other adult family members and friends come to despise one of the spouses and blame the divorce entirely on that person – and on his or her relatives and friends. And, as noted above, it's even common for professionals involved in a high-conflict divorce case to develop an extreme disrespect and disdain for each other, as they choose sides and support only their clients.

High-Conflict Emotions Are Highly Contagious

How does this happen? Recent brain research helps explain this process. It appears that we have two basic systems of conflict resolution associated with the right and left hemispheres of our brains. While the differences between the two hemispheres can be exaggerated, researchers are finding that these differences do exist (Schore, 2012). The left brain is mostly where written and spoken word content is processed. Most of the time, researchers say that our left hemisphere is dominant, working at problem-solving in a logical, detailed manner that is generally associated with positive emotions, such as calmness, contentment and a sense of safety. This is where we tend to store and reflect on specific detailed solutions to previous problems, which helps in planning logical and detailed solutions to new problems.

Our right brain tends to be more creative and intuitive. This is a good thing. But also, part of the right brain takes over when we are in a crisis or when we face a totally new situation, and it shuts down our logical problem-solving in favor of fast protective action with fight, flight or freeze responses. Such an approach helps to save our lives when facing an immediate, life-or-death problem.

This defensive response includes splitting: fast all-or-nothing thinking, intensely negative crisis emotions and extreme behaviors (running away, violently attacking, or trying to hide). The right brain unconsciously and constantly pays great attention to people's tone of voice and facial expressions. These emotional expressions are highly contagious during a crisis. Before you realize it, you may start reacting to a situation like those around you (running, fighting), in an effort to protect the group through shared strength. This group defense mechanism (contagious emotions) has saved humans for thousands of years. It's like emotional Wi-Fi (Goleman, 2006).

Before we developed written language (about 5,000 years ago), much of human communication depended on the accurate reading of facial expressions, tone of voice and hand gestures – all interpreted by the right hemisphere of our brains. Because this was just a tad before Google, you couldn't read up on the reliability of a group leader or the history of a group of strangers. Our right brains developed in such a way as to be able to read each other's good faith or bad faith intentions, just based on these non-verbal characteristics. So, how would we have reliably picked our leaders?

Interestingly, it appears that we may not have evolved as much as we had hoped. Research has found that most elections have resulted in choosing the candidate that looks more competent, regardless of his or her abilities. Researchers have shown photos of the candidates to panels of people who didn't know them and asked them to pick which candidate simply looked more competent. The results have shown that they select the person who was the winner in more than two-thirds of United States Senate and House elections. This research finding has also been demonstrated when using samples from other countries. When shown photos of the two candidates, *for only one second*, they still are able to guess accurately who won the election most of the time (Brooks, 2011).

We humans are constantly trying to figure out who to believe, who to follow and who to fight for.

So, it seems that our ancestor voters picked leaders based on their looks, other non-verbal cues and group opinion, rather than on what they said and what they stood for. This provided the potential to form stable communities in stable locations, with leaders that everyone mostly agreed to follow – until they were found to be wrong. Then, the next tallest, strongest, most persuasive, most competent-looking leader would come along and lead the revolution. We humans are constantly trying to figure out who to believe, who to follow and who to fight for. Thus, leaders have developed skills at convincing us, with very little logical information – for thousands of years!

So, our brains often make decisions based on information we are not consciously thinking about (conscious thinking seems more associated with the left brain). It's easy for us to get triggered into defensive, non-logical thinking based on the intense emotions of others (that's more of a right-brain activity). Here's how our two types of conflict resolution thinking tend to work:

2 Ways We Deal with Conflict

LOGICAL PROBLEM-SOLVING	FAST DEFENSIVE REACTING
Flexible thinking, many solutions	All-or-nothing solutions
Sees situation as a problem to solve	Sees situation as an extreme crisis
Situation requires a good logical analysis	Situation requires fast action, not analysis
The problem is complex, has many parts	The problem is simple; it's bad people
Sees self as open to improvement	Sees self as all good (you have to in crisis)
Sees problems in context of other issues	Sees problems in isolation from other issues
Sees compromise as normal part of life	Sees compromise as life-threatening
Wants to preserve benefits of relationship(s)	Sees no future relationship with the other(s)
Seeks others with information and ideas	Seeks others who will agree and fight
Fear and anger can be managed and should not interfere with making good decisions	Fear and anger are overwhelming and should drive quick, defensive action, NOW!

How do you decide which method to use?

This is partly decided by your environment and partly by you. You can't ignore your environment and its messages of potential danger. Are the people around you friend or enemy? Is the friendly person talking to you really a friendly person, or a sneaky person who poses a threat and might hurt you if you let him or her get too close?

The part of the brain that picks up threats from your environment is your "amygdala." It operates like a smoke detector. It grabs your attention in as few as 6 thousandths of a second and shuts everything else out of your mind. Researchers say that the amygdala in your right hemisphere (you have one in each hemisphere) is especially sensitive to other people's facial expressions of fear or anger. If your brain sees and hears an angry person, your amygdala will shut down your logical thinking and you will go into fight, flight or freeze mode.

...if you are facing a situation in which others are telling you that there is a crisis... it can be very hard to ignore, even for those with strong self-control....

Of course, you can override your amygdala response – with your pre-frontal cortex (located in the very front of your brain). This is your highest level of thinking and decision-making. In a sense, it is your control center. This is the last area of the brain to develop and the seat of one of the biggest projects of adolescence, namely, learning self-control. It's not fully developed until about age 25.

Someone with strong self-control can ignore many crisis signals and really choose which messages to ignore. But, if you are facing a situation in which others are telling you that there is a crisis – especially society's leaders, and especially over and over again with great fervor – it can be very hard to ignore, even for those with strong self-control.

Mirror Neurons

Another aspect of the brain that seems to contribute to the splitting dynamic is the "mirror neuron system." This was discovered within the past 15 years by Giacomo Rizzolatti and his research team in Italy and notably researched by UCLA neuroscientist, Marco Iacoboni (2008). Mirror neurons play out in our brains what we observe others do, as if we were doing the exact same action along with them. For example, while you are watching someone playing baseball, you are also at the exact same time playing baseball in your brain in the exact same way. Since these mirror neurons are often right next to action neurons ("motor neurons") in your brain, they appear to be helping you get ready to do what you see other people doing. If you had never played baseball before and the baseball suddenly came in your direction, you might automatically catch it and throw it back the same way – because your neurons had already been practicing and getting you ready to do the exact same actions. This appears to be a primary way that children learn.

This works the same way for emotions and is the presumed basis for empathy. When people – especially those we are close to or trust – show their emotions, we are very likely to mirror those emotions. For example, when a friend is smiling and tells us a funny story, we are likely to smile and laugh too. When a friend is sad or angry, we are likely to feel and show sadness and anger also. It's almost automatic.

Apparently, mirror neurons also imitate the human behavior we see on TV, in the movies and on our screens (computers, phones, tablets, etc.). The effect might not be as intense as it is when we are face-to-face with someone we know, but it still has this effect. When TV, movies and other screens show frightened or angry faces, we feel frightened or angry, and we are likely to show such emotions to others – unless we overrule them with our prefrontal cortex. But, who has time to overrule much of what you see on a screen with quick-paced, rapidly changing images, purposely edited to keep your rapt attention? We tend to digest it without even "thinking" consciously (with our left brain). With sufficient repetition, it becomes extremely hard to overrule the intense emotions that are elicited and driven by an actor's dramatic tone of voice, intense facial expressions and strong hand-gestures (that appeal to our right brain).

Moreover, we currently live in a culture of blame and disrespect.

Incivility and Bullying

The discovery of mirror neurons helps explain the rise in incivility and bullying we have seen over the past decade. Children live what they learn, especially what they see and hear! And, adults do too. In many ways, you become what you see and hear! Research even shows that those surrounded by over-weight people tend to become heavier; those around smokers become smokers; and those around happy people become happier (Brooks, 2011). We mirror our culture more than we actually "think" for ourselves. Moreover, we currently live in a culture of blame and disrespect. This is played out in family courts around the country and exemplified by the increase in high-conflict divorce. This is also increasingly being played out in our political elections.

Narcissistic Leaders

Another apparently unconscious and powerful expression of splitting is the behavior of narcissistic leaders. As mentioned at the beginning of this chapter, narcissistic personalities are one of the two most likely types to drive high-conflict divorce by seeing people as all-good or all-bad (Millon, 1996). They are particularly effective in their contagious effective in transmitting splitting to others.

We mirror our culture more than we actually "think" for ourselves.

Narcissists generally are self-absorbed, see themselves as superior (without good reason), lack empathy for others, and misjudge others (as overly weak or overly threatening). They are over-confident, but this tends to backfire. In the short-term, they persuade others to let them be the leaders. But, in the long-term, they are less successful than non-narcissistic leaders. Researchers studying narcissism conclude the following:

> ...overconfidence backfires. This makes some sense; narcissists are lousy at taking criticism and learning from mistakes. They also like to blame everyone and everything except themselves for their shortcomings. Second,

> they lack motivation to improve because they believe they have already made it: when you were born on home plate, why run around the bases? Third, overconfidence itself can lead to poor performance. If you think you know all of the answers, there's no need to study. Then you take the test and fail. Oops.
>
> Reprinted with the permission of The Free Press, a Division of Simon & Schuster, Inc., from *The Narcissism Epidemic: Living in the Age of Entitlement* by Jean M. Twenge and W. Keith Campbell.

In high-conflict divorce, narcissists (and borderlines) can be "highly persuasive blamers." This becomes a problem for family court, since many family court decisions are based on credibility. However, narcissists are skilled at appearing credible. Their confidence in their statements and their conviction in blaming others can be very convincing and contagious. As Eddy and Kreger (2011) wrote in their book, *Splitting: Protecting Yourself While Divorcing Someone with Borderline or Narcissistic Personality Disorder*, persuasive blamers promote splitting in family court, with the following behaviors:

- Blames a specific target (such as a partner, child, or professional) for feeling abandoned or inferior.
- Repeatedly attacks or blames the target with violence, verbal abuse, financial abuse, legal abuse, and so on.
- Sees target as all bad (splitting).

- Has extreme emotional intensity about blaming target.
- Launches personal attacks on target's intelligence and sanity.
- Preoccupied with analyzing target's character traits.
- Recruits others to attack target (negative advocates).
- Seeks other professionals to blame target.
- Seeks validation for own thinking and behavior.
- Seeks retaliation against target.
- Often sees court as most accessible source of power and control in our society.

In family court, these characteristics give narcissists a one-up in court decisions. Because they truly see themselves as superior, they can convince others that their target of blame is truly deficient or despicable (unfit mom; deadbeat dad; child molester; spousal abuser), when it is completely untrue. Or, they may actually engage in such abusive behavior and persuasively deny it to others – including lawyers, counselors, mediators, evaluators and judges. The credibility of narcissists in family court should not be based on their appearance of honesty and sincerity. Outside research and evaluation are necessary – just as they are in politics.

What Does Splitting Have to Do With Politics?

We have come to realize that splitting in politics is driven by the same high-conflict behaviors as in family court. And, the result is also the same!

The Five Drivers of Political Splitting

1. Personal attacks (it's about their morals, intelligence, sanity, etc., not the issue).

2. Crisis emotions (such as fear and anger, which trigger fear and hatred).

3. All-or-nothing solutions (such as eliminating a person or group).

4. Narcissistic behavior (saying you are a hero, while not really showing empathy for anyone else).

5. Negative advocates (recruiting others, such as Super PACs and attack ad consultants).

If you are willing to engage in splitting, you can get very far – until enough people understand this dynamic and set limits on it.

And, there is a lot of repetition, which strengthens the splitting and gives it the appearance of appropriate behavior and widespread acceptance.

In addition, the Four Key Players are the same in politics as in family court:

The Four Key Players of Splitting (in Divorce and in Politics)

1. High-conflict person (HCP) or someone engaged in high-conflict behavior.

2. Negative advocates (who endorse, defend and promote the HCP's thinking, emotions and behavior – no matter how bad).

3. A public forum (such as family court or the news media).

4. Bystanders (who the HCP or the other upset person try to persuade to become advocates; in the case of politics, it is the voters).

The winner is the person that collects the most negative advocates and/or the most persuasive negative advocates. What follows is a comparative chart of how it is playing out today in high-conflict divorce and in high-conflict elections.

Similarity of High-Conflict Divorce and Elections

HIGH-CONFLICT DIVORCE	HIGH-CONFLICT ELECTIONS
One or both parents are engaging in high-conflict behavior in the divorce: • Using intense negative arguments. • Trying to eliminate the other parent from any role in the child's life. • Presenting the other as a completely bad person. • Repeating this over and over. • Having extreme statements and behavior tolerated by Family Court and professionals, which gives the appearance of public acceptance.	One or both candidates are engaging in high-conflict behavior in public: • Using intense emotional speeches. • Trying to eliminate the other candidate/party from any public role. • Presenting the other as a completely bad person. • Repeating this over and over. • Having extreme statements and behaviors tolerated by News Media and other politicians, which give the appearance of public acceptance.
An HCP parent recruits negative advocates, including family, friends and professionals, to continually repeat intense blame of the evil other.	An HCP candidate recruits negative advocates, including powerful friends and professionals, to continually repeat intense blame of the evil other.
The professionals may include highly paid lawyers to develop personal attack strategies.	The professionals may include highly paid agencies to develop personal attack ads.

Similarity of High-Conflict Divorce and Elections Cont.

HIGH-CONFLICT DIVORCE	HIGH-CONFLICT ELECTIONS
The personal attacks will be very fast and brief, so that they are emotionally persuasive and not challenged by accurate information.	The personal attacks will be very fast and brief, so that they are emotionally persuasive and not challenged by accurate information.
The personal attacks will be presented as a fight of good against evil (child molester, alienator), triggering amygdala and shutting down logic.	The personal attacks will be presented as a fight of good against evil (capitalism, socialism), triggering amygdala and shutting down logic.
A problem-solving spouse or parent won't adequately defend self because he or she is a natural problem-solver, not a natural blamer.	A problem-solving candidate won't adequately defend self because he or she is a natural problem-solver, not a natural blamer.
The child, as bystander, may absorb the emotional intensity, all-or-nothing solutions, and personal attacks and come to believe that the less aggressive parent is actually evil and dangerous; this child will come to hate that parent and refuse to have any contact.	The voters, as bystanders, may absorb the emotional intensity, all-or-nothing solutions, and personal attacks and come to believe that the less aggressive candidate is actually evil and dangerous; these voters will come to hate that candidate and vote against him or her.

The Rest of this Book

With this background of how the same splitting dynamic drives high-conflict divorce and high-conflict politics today, the rest of this book examines the four Key Players in the electoral process, in order to demonstrate the strength of this similarity and what can be done about it. Our goal is not to take "sides" in this process, but instead to show how powerfully destructive this high-conflict splitting dynamic can be. If we, as a nation, don't learn how to contain it, it will certainly destroy our national family, as surely as it has destroyed millions of divorcing families over the past 20-30 years.

"I think it was an election year."

Chapter 4

How High-Conflict Politicians Turn Peace Into War

High-conflict people tend to turn peace into war, regardless of the setting they are in. They naturally see the world in highly adversarial terms. They really trust no one except themselves and frequently turn against their own friends and family. However, they can also be extremely charming and persuasive, as we have explained is part of the splitting dynamic.

They repeatedly sound the alarm of great danger and then persuade many people that they are the only heroes who can rescue them (the children in high-conflict divorce, or the voters in high-conflict elections) from this great danger. The only problem is that the great danger may be non-existent, or quite exaggerated. Moreover, rather than actually being great heroes, they tend to have serious problems of their own which they don't recognize. Whether in divorce or in politics, beware of the charm and the

"I'll-fight-for-you" statements proclaimed by the HCPs. Always ask: *Is it really a crisis? Is this really a hero?*

Relationship Conflict Skills

In a relationship, the skills you use to resolve conflicts require the ability to protect both the relationship and yourself. You need to have a balance. If you blow a hole in the other person's end of the boat, you'll both sink. Think of it as relationships needing a "surge protector," similar to the one you have for your computer. They function to protect you from getting fried by a sudden power surge. You can be angry at your partner, but you can't be too angry for too long. You can say awful things in the heat of the argument, but you better make up soon or you risk destroying your future security with this friend or family member.

This issue has been studied by marriage researchers. Two of the most respected and well-known experts on this subject are John and Julia Gottman. They have studied what makes marriages succeed or fail. After only a 15-minute video interview with married couples who are hooked up to monitors that measure heart rate and electrical conductivity of the skin, the Gottmans can predict with over 90% accuracy whether the marriage is likely to end in divorce.

They have discovered that one of the characteristics of a healthy marriage is that there is a five-to-one (5:1) ratio of positive interactions to negative interactions. This apparently holds true both for couples who bicker a lot, and for quiet couples who rarely seem to argue. Because the happily married bickerers have so many more positive interactions than negative interactions, they can tolerate their many petty arguments (5:1). The quiet couples don't seem to argue much, but their ratio is apparently 5:1, as well. They don't seem to need as many positive interactions as the bickerers, because they don't have as many of the negative interactions to counteract. (Gottman, 1994)

When high-conflict couples get divorced, however, the high-conflict person (HCP) often switches to putting out no positive and 100% negative interactions, comments and behaviors. This significantly escalates the conflict and prevents it from being resolved or resolvable. Much of the difficulty of high-conflict divorce is getting the HCP (or two HCPs) to see enough positive in the other person to be able to reach agreements and let go of the conflicts.

HCPs are the ones who take the fight, rather than the flight or freeze approach.

This reasonable awareness is not natural for HCPs, once they are in a highly defensive state (right brain defensiveness). Instead, they have the all-or-nothing thinking associated with this defensiveness. They often cannot calm themselves enough to reach their left-brain problem-solving abilities, so they, instead, remain stuck in their fight, flight or freeze defensiveness. HCPs are the ones who take the fight, rather than the flight or freeze, approach.

In politics, this turns into entirely negative statements about the other candidate or party, so that those who only listen to one side grow to hate the evil-other. If the politicians have nothing positive to say, then the other side must be extreme and self-protective. The message is consistently one of crisis, so that the listener's fear and anger response will override and shut down their logical analysis and block any search for real information.

The Issue is Not the Issue

As we mentioned in Chapter Two, some high-conflict disputes have one high-conflict person (HCP), while others have two HCPs, and still others have two ordinarily "reasonable" people who become caught up in a high-conflict environment that pushes them into high-conflict behavior. This behavior may be foreign to them, but it feels necessary to them and to those around them. Politicians seem to fit into these same three categories.

> *With HCPs, the issue is not the issue - their personality is the issue.*

With HCPs, the issue is not the issue – their *personality* is the issue. If you solve one problem in dealing with them, another will just take its place. The high-conflict person will just keep fighting, blaming, thinking only of him or herself, and contributing more to the problem than to the solution. HCPs don't seem to learn from their mistakes. This appears to be true, regardless of the setting. When you're dealing with an HCP, this is the predictable dynamic, once you know what to look for, whether it's in divorce or in politics.

In divorce and other legal disputes, a high-conflict person (HCP) tends to have the following 10 characteristics that drive the conflict higher and higher, rather than that reduce or resolve it (Eddy, 2006):

1. Is rigid and uncompromising.
2. Repeats failed strategies.
3. Is unable to accept and heal loss.
4. Makes everything personal.

5. Has emotions that dominate his or her thinking.
6. Is unable to reflect on his or her own behavior.
7. Avoids responsibility for the problem or solution.
8. Is preoccupied with blaming others.
9. Draws others into the disputes ("negative advocates").
10. Can look really good for a few months (intelligent, attractive, charming, persuasive).

Do any (or all) of these fit politicians? Let's look at some recent examples:

In 2006, the District Attorney near Duke University, Michael Nifong, loudly accused three students of raping a young woman from the nearby neighborhood, in a high profile case (he was running for re-election at the time) and he blamed Duke for tolerating this behavior among its athletes. Soon, everyone was angry at Duke and its athletes. Rallies were held. This D.A. was extremely loud, blaming, – and wrong! He ignored the forensic evidence that showed it could not have been the students, and eventually he lost his license to practice law in North Carolina because of his extremely unethical and high-conflict behavior.

In New York, in 2008, Eliot Spitzer, a governor with a reputation for being extremely difficult to work with, stepped down after it was revealed that he was a client in a prostitution ring. He might have escaped having to resign his office, except that he had alienated far too many people with his high-conflict behavior in his first year as Governor and previously as the New York Attorney General.

More recently, in 2009, there was the Governor of Illinois, Rod Blagojevich, who was impeached and thrown out of office by a unanimous vote of the state legislature. He was convicted of corruption charges and sent to prison. He demonstrated the arrogance of an office-holder who didn't seem to believe that the rules applied to him. This reminds us of the narcissism research described in the last chapter.

Of course, we can't leave out President Bill Clinton's affair with Monica Lewinsky while he was in the White House in 1998. It reached the point that he was impeached by the House of Representatives (charged with violating federal laws for lying to investigators) but was then acquitted. He was able to stay in office, but he, too, seemed to believe that the rules didn't apply to him, so that he could self-justify having taken such chances.

Too much narcissism means that you believe you are more important than your relationships.

Speaking of narcissism, there was the case against Presidential candidate, John Edwards, in 2012. He was prosecuted on charges of violating federal campaign laws by spending nearly $1 million of donors' money on hiding his affair with his mistress (and their love-child). While eventually he was found not guilty, he admitted that he was guilty of narcissism:

> "[My experiences] fed a self-focus, an egotism, a narcissism that leads you to believe you can do whatever you want." He admitted that he had become 'increasingly egocentric and narcissistic'. (ABC News, Aug. 12, 2008)

Too much narcissism means that you believe you are more important than your relationships. A narcissistic politician doesn't care what anyone else thinks – he (or she) already knows all the "right" answers. Such a politician doesn't need to listen to the "other side" and seek compromises for the greater good. He (or she) already knows what the greater good is, in his (or her) own mind. What will benefit him is what will be best for the U.S.A., their thinking goes. And, he honestly believes this. That's one of the benefits of narcissism – self-delusion. It works for a while and actually helps the narcissist persuade others to agree that he (or she) is God's gift to the world. Unfortunately, it doesn't last. Narcissists are actually worse at meeting their goals and interpreting reality. But, it takes a while to figure that out. It often is after an election, but it could be before.

High-conflict politicians seem preoccupied with telling you how wonderful they are and what they will do – all on their own – when they are in power. They speak in all-or-nothing terms: "I will eliminate this department. I will declare war on that waste. I will bring America back from the evil-others who want to harm us." This could be HCPs on the right or on the left. You have to listen closely to the terms they use, not which side they are on. HCPs on either side are a problem, although at different times in history they seem to be more on one side or the other.

War and Narcissism

Those who study war and terrorism see these same dynamics. A book by a former FBI Special Agent, Joe Navarro, describes the relevance of splitting and narcissism to terrorist leaders. He explains that "psychological splitting" is a common characteristic. "No matter how good things have been, the minute something goes wrong, or there is a shift of allegiance, the person psychologically "splits" and totally devalues the other person... The ability to switch so suddenly and irrevocably had been noted in many terrorists... When it comes to terrorism, narcissism is perhaps one of the most often observed traits" (Navarro, 2005).

Mr. Navarro mentions that Saddam Hussein likely fit this category and described how contemptuous Saddam was after he was caught during the Iraq war. He also demonstrated another important and self-defeating characteristic about narcissists, which is that they tend to misjudge other people at the same time as they are misjudging themselves. They think they know how the other person (or political leader) thinks, feels and will act. A good description of this mistake of judgment by Saddam, which led to the war in Iraq, is described in George W. Bush's autobiography (2010) regarding events after Saddam was captured:

> *If Saddam didn't have WMD [weapons of mass destruction], why wouldn't he just prove it to the inspectors? Every psychological profile I had read told me Saddam was a survivor. If he cared so much about staying in power, why would he gamble his regime by pretending to have?*
>
> *Part of the explanation came after Saddam's capture, when he was de-briefed by the FBI. He told agents that he was more worried about looking weak to Iran than being removed by the coalition. He never thought the United States would follow through on our promises to disarm him by force. I'm not sure what more I could have done to show Saddam I meant what I said (p. 260).*

In other words, Saddam assumed that President Bush was thinking like he was - bluffing. He was hinting that he had weapons of mass destruction to look big and strong, and he apparently thought that Bush was just trying to look big and strong, too.

But President Bush responded like someone mirroring an HCP. He, too, appears to have misjudged Saddam, by thinking that Saddam was thinking like he was – that the United States had substantial weapons and intended to use them. The subsequent invasion of Iraq turned out to be based on many misjudgments on both sides such as these, and turned into one of the longest wars in U.S. history.

Perhaps a tendency toward all-or-nothing thinking played a part in some of these decisions. In his autobiography, President Bush (2010) mentions the decision by his Ambassador to Iraq (Jerry Bremer) to exclude members of Saddam's political party after the invasion in 2003, and the response to it:

> *Forming the Governing Council was an important way to demonstrate that Saddam's tyranny was gone forever. With that in mind, Jerry issued two orders shortly after his arrival in Baghdad. One declared that certain members of Saddam's Baath Party would not be eligible to serve in the new government of Iraq. The other formally disbanded the Iraqi army, which had largely disappeared on its own.*
>
> *In some ways, the orders achieved their objectives. Iraq's Shia and Kurds—the majority of the population—welcomed the clean break from Saddam. But the orders had a psychological impact I did not foresee. Many Sunnis took them as a signal they would have*

no place in Iraq's future. This was especially dangerous in the case of the army. Thousands of armed men had just been told they were not wanted. Instead of signing up for the new military, many joined the insurgency.

In retrospect, I should have insisted on more debate on Jerry's orders, especially on what message disbanding the army would send and how many Sunnis the de-Baathification would affect (p. 259).

We have empathy for President Bush, as we can't imagine what it must have been like to be president on September 11, 2001. Who could have imagined that any group of people would kill themselves by flying jets into tall buildings? No one had ever dealt with that reality before. We don't know if he is an HCP or not. However, his responses may have been a good example of mirroring HCPs. This includes the all-or-nothing language that entered into the world's vocabulary soon after that event. In his State of the Union address in January, 2002, he spoke of threats posed by Iraq, Iran and North Korea.

"States like these, and their terrorist allies, constitute an axis of evil, arming to threaten the peace of the world," I said. The media seized on the phrase 'axis of evil'" (p. 233).

Whether it was his repeated use of this phrase or the media's extreme repetition, this term itself represented an escalation of conflict worldwide. It also coincided with a significant increase in bullying at home, with more people seeing each other as evil in many of their relationships over the past decade. Perhaps this is a good example of the spreading of splitting.

In his autobiography, even President Bush said that he may have made some statements that were unwisely provocative. "I learned from the experience and paid close attention to how I communicated with each audience in the years ahead" (Bush, 2010, p. 261). We believe this is an important lesson for everyone for the years ahead, for politicians and everyone else, so that we don't inadvertently mirror HCPs.

The Problem with *WarSpeak* at Home

You might say or think that it's just harmless politicking when politicians use war language for addressing ordinary political problems. You might figure that everyone knows it's not to inspire actual violence. However, with the splitting dynamic, we are seeing more interpersonal violence.

In high-conflict divorces, we are seeing more and more murder-suicides in the news, increasingly including the death of the children. Whether these cases are truly increasing, or it's just the news media more dramatically high-lighting these tragedies, it's hard to know. However, the disturbed thinking in many of these cases seems to be influenced by the increasingly public commentary about all-or-nothing thinking and blaming attached to high-conflict divorce. Some of these murderous parents even make statements suggesting that they had to kill the children to protect them from an even worse life in the other parent's care, or even directly protect them from the evil other parent!

When public figures, such as Dr. Phil on a TV program in April, 2011, say things like "family court is broken" and that he will do something about it, this seems to suggest that vigilante justice is a valid response, because our institutions are "failing." When parents kidnap their children, they usually say they are the "protective" parent; protecting their children from the evil system. They are encouraged by such public extreme statements about institutions failing.

But is this really a crisis? Is this really a hero? Or, are these sorts of "protective" parents really HCPs who truly believe that they know better than everyone else what is best for their children, despite what professionals and judges might say, who have a larger picture of the issues involved in a particular case? Certainly, our institutions, including family courts, always need re-assessment and reform of their procedures and knowledge-base, but all-or-nothing statements about them don't help – they just feed public disrespect and dangerous self-help approaches.

When Gabby Giffords was shot and several others were killed in Tucson, Arizona, in 2011, there had been a recent series of well-publicized political statements and images promoting a war-like environment. One high-profile politician publicized politicians "in the cross-hairs" of a gun, as a way of saying which candidates needed to be defeated. To what extent that encouraged the mentally disturbed person who shot Gabby Giffords, we will never know for sure. But it seems that such high-conflict rhetoric (emotional, all-or-nothing solutions, highly blaming) is a contributing factor when it is repeated often enough – and it appears to be repeated more dramatically during recent elections.

In the 1960s, the war-like rhetoric about ending the Vietnam War also seemed to drive violence at home. The Weather Underground organization and others justified bombing buildings in an effort to stop the war. People were injured and some killed (even if that wasn't their intent), in response to some of the extreme rhetoric from the left, at that time.

When Timothy McVeigh blew up the Murrah Federal Building in Oklahoma City in 1995, he saw himself as a hero fighting an over-reaching federal government. Even though he killed many daycare children in the building, as well as government workers, he justified it with a cause that he himself defined. But it was encouraged by the warspeak of anti-government militias at the time, who saw themselves as somehow under attack from the federal government.

Remember, we are not concluding that this is a problem of the left or of the right.

We also have those who have killed doctors that perform abortions, who justify their actions by the wide-spread rhetoric against abortion, which more recently includes bloody messages and high-intensity emotions. Yes, abortion is a concern, but, if people don't agree with one another, is this the solution? Taking matters into one's own hands seems to be the response of some individuals (usually disturbed) to high-conflict political statements. In other words, words are not harmless when promoted by highly emotional arguments, all-or-nothing solutions and personalization – especially when they are repeated over and over again by HCPs. *Is this really a crisis? Is this really a hero?*

Remember, we are not concluding that this is a problem of the left or of the right. This is a problem of high-conflict individuals and their negative advocates, who go too far in their splitting rhetoric – which poses dangerous risks to our country as a whole. We have to remember that we are the most heavily armed country in the world, with the latest estimates that there are at least as many handguns as there are people in our country. Our language has matched the increase in weapons with our increase in expressions of war. Since 9/11, we have simply added more wars to our language of problem-solving: the War on Terror…the War on Drugs…the War on Poverty…the War on Illiteracy…the War on Obesity…the War on … (you fill in the blank). Our TV political debate programs have such names as "Cross-fire," "Hardball," "Rapid Fire," all apparently aimed to stimulate viewers' aggressive tendencies for entertainment.

Perhaps through the contagion effect, such high-conflict language has even filtered down to our daily conversations about sports. When a team wins, you now hear, "We killed them!" or "We slayed them!" Even in entertainment, this type of martial language is used. For example, on the TV show, American Idol, when a performer does well on a song, the judges say things like, "You killed it!" or "That was a killer performance," or "That was so great, I want to punch you!" And, even in facilitating positive relationships, we say "I killed him with kindness." This violent mind-set seems to be a very disturbing trend.

Making it Personal

Have you noticed how very personal election rhetoric has become? "Obamacare" does not appear to be an accidental term chosen by opponents of the Affordable Healthcare Act. It has now been repeated thousands – perhaps millions – of times, thanks to today's endless news cycle. If you ask people who already hate Obamacare why they hate it, they often don't know – just like alienated children in a high-conflict divorce who don't know why hate their mother or father. They just do! The more likely reason is that they have been exposed to the splitting dynamic, which is emotionally absorbed rather than logically analyzed, because:

It is **personal** – by attaching the President's name, it is a short-cut to showing disdain for the President that you can deny is disdain for the President.

It is said with **crisis emotions** – often with disdain.

It is described with **all-or-nothing** solutions – it is "all-bad" and the only solution is to eliminate it.

It is **preoccupied with blaming others** – it is ALL his fault; it represents the take-over of America; it is the end of life as we know it; it is socialism; next, he will force you to eat broccoli.

It is **repeated endlessly** in the media – the term "Obamacare" has been repeated 24/7 for over 3 years, as of this writing.

While this may be more characteristic of the Right today, those on the Left were similarly extreme in the 1960s and 1970s in their hateful rhetoric about Presidents Johnson and Nixon. During the Vietnam War, one of the popular slogans directed toward President Johnson was "Hey hey, LBJ, how many kids did you kill today?" And, Richard Nixon was described as "Tricky Dick." Actually, over 50,000 young American soldiers were killed in that war, but does this justify building hatred for the person, rather than making policy changes? Such language has blocked, rather than promoted dialogue.

Some would say that none of today's "crises" compare to the crises in those times – yet the extreme statements repeatedly heard today in the 24-hour news cycle make today's situation seem worse than what was seen once a day on the 6:00 p.m. news with Walter Cronkite. Ironically, despite 24/7 news, the remaining wars of the present in Iraq and Afghanistan barely receive any news coverage anymore, yet young soldiers are still dying.

One would believe that Obamacare was worse than the Vietnam War, based on exposure to the emotional intensity, the all-or-nothing thinking, and the extreme blaming in today's 24-hour reporting. Our guess is that there are people today who hate Obama as much as, or even more, than people hated Johnson and Nixon. Yet they don't know what Obamacare even contains. This is how right-brain defensiveness is stoked through repeated fear and anger. It's not logical, because intense fear and anger shut down logical analysis.

Perhaps the personal nature of the attacks from the left against him led Johnson (previously the hero of the civil rights movement of liberals) to choose not to run for re-election in 1968. By 1970, the intensity of war rhetoric and hatred from both sides about the Vietnam War may have been a significant factor in the tension that led to the shooting of 4 students at a demonstration at Kent State University in Ohio. The splitting dynamic of fear and hatred can fuel emotional responses that override logic and reason and lead to violence. Do we want to return to this type of split in America?

Of course, the best example of personalization and the splitting dynamic by an HCP was the generation of hatred so well-trained by Adolf Hitler. He taught Germans to blame Jews, via radio speeches that had intense negative emotions, all-or-nothing solutions (the holocaust), the personalization of a group (actually several groups: Jews, gays, gypsies and others), and the endless repetition of his speeches on the radio. This wasn't just something he liked to do – it was essential in unifying the German people around his hate-based policies, which probably could not have gone far without him constantly pumping them up.

He cleverly got the German people, from the youngest children on up, to actively participate in rallies, songs, and movies – all repeating his emotion-based message of blame and hatred. They learned to hate weak minorities, with no basis in fact for their beliefs. Yet, it had the power to drive a whole continent – and the United States – into World War II. Was there a crisis in Germany after World War I? Yes, there was an economic crisis. Was Hitler the hero he claimed to be? Absolutely not. Yet, he fooled a nation for nearly 15 years. In Germany, there is a parade center exhibit about the Nazis that displays photos representing the emotional hysteria Hitler was able to generate, from the early 1930's until the end of World War II in 1945. It graphically shows how he went from a common criminal in the early 1930s to a master manipulator of a nation, by generating hate rhetoric and displays in the news – using the radio, movies and newsreels.

Lack of Self-Restraint

The increase of HCPs in today's politics is partially the result of several big changes in political speech over the past fifty years. Politicians weren't always so free in their public criticisms of each other, and the rules didn't allow such statements to go without a response.

Prior to about 1970, candidates were really chosen by party leaders, mostly out of sight of the public – somewhere in a "smoke-filled back room." Primaries were less significant, and conventions were for the crowning of the candidates, after a lot of haggling behind the scenes. Party leaders gained power by leading and working with other politicians in large local and national organizations. Private criticism and public praise helped politicians progress through the ranks and earn their candidacies.

In the 1970's, the rules changed to allow for more open political conventions and much more public participation in choosing a candidate. Young people, who had been politically active against the Vietnam War, helped nominate George McGovern as the Democratic candidate in 1972. This turned out to be a disaster for the Democratic Party, as the Republican candidate, Richard Nixon, won all but one state. But, the trend of party activists driving the selection of party candidates began to grow into what you see today, with candidates courting the most hard-core party activists in the primaries, then trying to shift gears toward the center, after their conventions.

You don't have to be a narcissist to be successful, but Americans can think of lots of successful narcissists because they're always grabbing the limelight.

With direct elections (well, almost direct; don't forget the technicalities of the Electoral College made up of state representatives), popular participation has replaced back-room politics. But this also has led to advertising as the primary mechanism for reaching voters, rather than personal contact through precinct-walkers and community organizations.

Thus, we have seen the shift from candidates who are skilled at politics, to candidates who are skilled at self-promotion and getting attention. In other words, bring on the narcissistic HCPs!

Narcissists and Self-Promotion

In *The Narcissism Epidemic*, Jean Twenge and Keith Campbell (2009) have the following to say about narcissists and self-promotion:

We don't deny that self-promotion is now necessary in a world of increasing competition and decreasing loyalty. We have both advised some of our own graduate students to be more self-promoting in order to advance their careers. However, it is possible to be self-promoting when necessary without becoming completely narcissistic.

....

Another reason so many people believe that narcissists are phenomenally successful is that narcissists seek attention. In short, they're really good at getting on TV (or looking snazzy at the local bar, or showing off at the gym).

....

This phenomenon is easy to see in the media. Donald Trump, who puts his name on everything he builds, has his own TV show, named a university after himself (yes, there is a Trump University), and picks fights with talk show hosts, is a great example of someone who is both successful and appears to be narcissistic. We know about Donald Trump's success because he is relentlessly self-promoting. It is hard to miss The Donald in the media, and he is rich – but there are other real estate tycoons you've never heard of because they are not self-promoters and don't want to be in the limelight. For example, Warren Buffet, the billionaire investor, gave most of his fortune to charity and drives around Nebraska in a Lincoln with license plates that say THRIFTY. Tom Hanks, who has won two Best Actor Academy Awards, is

> known in the film industry for being a genuinely nice person, as was Paul Newman, who donated millions to charity. You don't have to be a narcissist to be successful, but Americans can think of lots of successful narcissists because they're always grabbing the limelight (pp. 83-85).
>
>

Yet, as leaders, they actually aren't great. Here are more comments by Twenge and Campbell (2009):

> It's tempting to believe that narcissism might still be beneficial when leading a large company. Not so, according to Jim Collins, the author of the bestselling business book, Good to Great. In an exhaustive study, Collins found that companies that moved from being "merely good to truly great" did so because they had what he calls "Level 5" leaders. These CEOs are not the charismatic, ultra-confident figures you would expect. Instead, they are humble, avoid the limelight, never rest on their laurels, and continuously try to prove themselves. Collins profiles Darwin E. Smith, the former CEO of Kimberly-Clark, who wore cheap suits and shunned publicity. In his twenty years of service as CEO, Smith oversaw stock returns that bested the market four times over. Instead of showing in-your-face braggadocio, Smith quietly kept at his work...

> ...The profile of the humble but determined CEO came up over and over. These CEOs were also excellent team players, something else narcissists aren't....
>
> In other words, Collins found that the best corporate leaders were not narcissistic or even particularly self-confident. Companies with short-term success, however, were often headed by attention-seeking, arrogant leaders. In these companies, Collins writes, "we noticed the presence of a gargantuan ego that contributed to the demise or continued mediocrity of the company." This lines up well with the academic research on narcissism and judgment: in the end, narcissists' overconfidence undermines their performance (p. 44).

But not all narcissists are high-conflict people. It tends to be the narcissistic politicians that are good at getting attention, have the big egos, arrogantly blow their own horns, and who engage in the splitting dynamic, that are high-conflict. They are the ones who do not restrain themselves from the behaviors that perpetuate splitting and hatred.

But narcissistic HCPs and others cannot do it all on their own. They really seek and often find a lot of negative advocates that will give them credibility and advance their "cause" (namely, themselves). The next chapter shows how this appears to apply in politics and is being brought to a new level never before seen in this country – just as high-conflict divorce continues to escalate to a new level of splitting.

"I got it from a super pac, I don't know where the hell they got it."

Chapter
5

Super PACs as Negative Advocates

Today's politicians need to directly and quickly persuade voters to elect them or to re-elect them. They don't have much time. They have to grab them, or they will lose. This process of persuasion is similar in many ways to that of parties in family court. Negative statements get much more attention and are more likely to "win" than are positive statements. Emotional arguments, rather than factual arguments seem to work better, when there's a short time-frame available. See the table on the following page for examples of the kinds of statements made in each.

Of course, these are the kinds of statements that HCPs say about each other all the time. To make it more powerful, and to escalate the tribal warfare, negative advocates can say these things with more authority and more repetition.

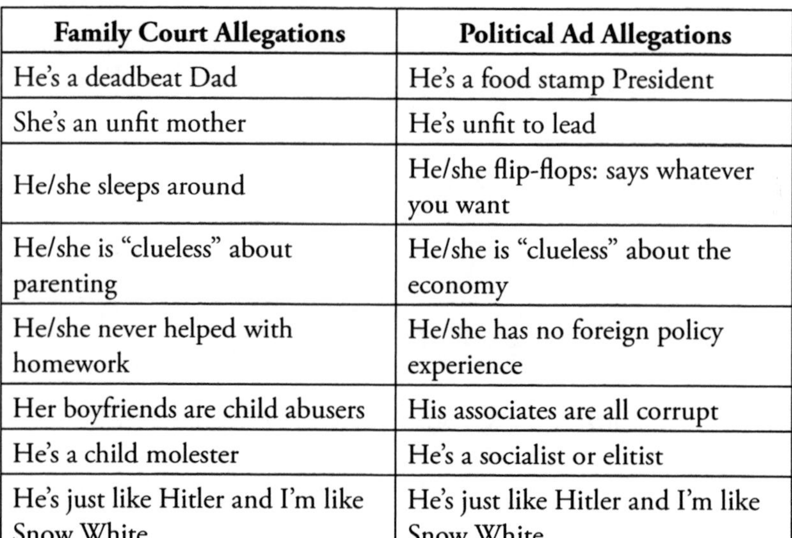

Family Court Allegations	Political Ad Allegations
He's a deadbeat Dad	He's a food stamp President
She's an unfit mother	He's unfit to lead
He/she sleeps around	He/she flip-flops: says whatever you want
He/she is "clueless" about parenting	He/she is "clueless" about the economy
He/she never helped with homework	He/she has no foreign policy experience
Her boyfriends are child abusers	His associates are all corrupt
He's a child molester	He's a socialist or elitist
He's just like Hitler and I'm like Snow White	He's just like Hitler and I'm like Snow White

In family court, the leading roles are given to family lawyers, psychological experts, and a parade of friends and family who come to testify about how the other party or parent is a real jerk. Judges have to put a lot of energy into restricting who can testify and what they can talk about. Hearing that Mary's mother thinks Tom is a jerk is useless. It is already assumed she will say that.

But, seeing a well-respected lawyer or psychologist in a suit can be very persuasive. If you have enough money, you can almost always find some professional who will say you are great and the other person is incompetent. While the vast majority of family lawyers and psychological experts are responsible and try to reduce and resolve conflicts, there are the 10% or so who will do and say almost anything for pay. These are the ones you hear the most about. For those with unlimited funds, high-conflict divorces can go on for years – in some cases much longer than the marriages themselves!

Super PACs and Politicians

Another major player in high-conflict politics is the Super Pacs. While they are heavily involved in today's elections, they have been around for years, but with some restrictions. "Soft money" was the term use to describe the contributions that wealthy people, companies and unions would make to their parties, even though there were restrictions on contributing to the specific candidates. And, these contributions were made fairly equally to both parties, up until the year 2000.

If you have enough money, you can almost always find some professional who will say you are great and the other person is incompetent.

In 2002, the Bipartisan Campaign Reform Act, more commonly known as the McCain-Feingold law (jointly sponsored by Republican John McCain and Democrat Russ Feingold), put an end to soft money raised and used by the parties. But it didn't prevent politicians and their advocates from creating new organizations outside of the parties, such as tax exempt "527" social welfare organizations. These outside groups were still limited in when and how they could spend their money – such as forbidding attack ads by outside organizations within 60 days of a general election.

Then, in 2010, the United States Supreme Court decided the case of Citizens United v. Federal Election Commission. This case expanded the rights of these outside groups to run their ads any time and provided the ability to accept corporate contributions. A recent analysis (Bai, 2012) explains the impact of these changes:

[After McCain-Feingold in 2002] The parties could no longer tap an endless stream of soft money, but thanks to the advent of the 527, rich ideologues with their own agendas could write massive checks for the purpose of building what were, essentially, shadow parties – independent groups with their own turnout and advertising campaigns, limited in what they could say but accountable to no candidate or party boss. Wealthy liberals like Soros and Lewis, along with groups like MoveOn.org, were the first to spot the opportunity. All told, wealthy liberals spent something close to $200 million in an effort to oust George W. Bush in 2004, setting an entirely new standard for outside spending.

....

[After Citizens United in 2010] Conservative groups alone, including a super PAC led by Karl Rove and another group backed by the brothers Charles and David Koch, will likely spend more than a billion dollars trying to take down Barack Obama by the time November rolls around.

....

[But] The greatest impact of this year's imbalance in outside money will be felt on the state level, where a lot of House seats and control of the Senate hang in the balance, and where a sharp gust of advertising can often blow the results in one direction or another.

But today it's much easier to tap into the fury and anxiety of out-of-power millionaires than it is to

> amass contributions in defense of the status quo. This dynamic probably explains why wealthy Democrats who pioneered the idea of outside money during the Bush years have largely stood down this year, even while conservative fund-raising has soared. It isn't that liberals don't like Obama or grow queasy at the mention of super PACs. It's a function of human nature: nobody really gets pumped up to write a $10 million check just to keep things more or less as they are.
>
> If you're a Democrat, there's some good news here. One persistent fear you hear from liberals is that Citizens United altered the balance between the parties in a permanent way – that corporate money will give Republicans a structural advantage that can never be overcome. What's more likely is that the boom in outside money will prove to be cyclical, with the momentum swinging toward whoever feels shut out and persecuted at the moment. Liberals dominated outside spending in 2004 and 2006. And should Romney become President, they'll most likely do so again (Bai, 2012).

This last comment fits high-conflict divorce exactly: when one side loses, that side gears up much stronger for the next round. You see, high-conflict divorce never ends. You can always come back to court to ask for a change in child custody or a modification of a child support order. In politics, it's like campaigning for the next election the day after, rather than accepting a loss.

So, there it is! An outright prediction in the national press: elections – presidential, state and local – will become driven by wealthy advocates, swinging back and forth from election to election - first one side, then the other. Does this sound different from the high-conflict Hollywood divorce we mentioned at the beginning of this chapter? Remember that the Hollywood case was only brought under control when the court required the parties to share power and time with their daughter.

But does money really bring an advantage in political elections?

Do Attack Ads Really Work?

The recent ad history goes back to the election of George H. W. Bush over Michael Dukakis in 1988, and the "Willie Horton ad" created by Larry McCarthy. In recent overview of this issue, Jane Mayer (2012) explained as follows:

> Paid for by a political group officially acting separately from the campaign of George H. W. Bush, it was the political equivalent of an improvised explosive device, demolishing the electoral hopes of Dukakis, then the governor of Massachusetts. Its key image was a mug shot of Horton—a scowling black man with a disheveled Afro. Horton, a convicted murderer, had escaped while on a weekend pass issued by a Massachusetts furlough program. A decade earlier, Dukakis had vetoed a bill that would have forbidden furloughs for murderers. After escaping, Horton raped a white woman and stabbed her fiancé. McCarthy knew that showing Horton's menacing face would make voters feel viscerally that Dukakis was soft on crime. Critics said

that the ad stoked racial fears, presenting a little-known black man as an icon of American violence.

McCarthy's ad was condemned at the time, by Democrats and Republicans, for exceeding the boundaries of civility. And it raised unsettling new questions about possibly unlawful coordination between an official campaign and an outside political group. In retrospect, the spot was not an aberration; both in its tone and in its murky origins, it created a blueprint for the future.

....

According to Floyd Brown, the conservative operative who hired McCarthy in 1988, the Horton ad "was incredibly effective." Brown maintains that Dukakis's lead over George H. W. Bush collapsed after the ad began airing. Tony Fabrizio, a Republican pollster and strategist who also worked on the Horton ad, argues that McCarthy was relatively restrained—there were no photographs of Horton's victims, for example. And Brown says that the ad became a scapegoat after Dukakis lost. Both men use the word "brilliant" to describe McCarthy. "Larry is not just one of the best ad-makers these days," Brown says. "He's one of the best advertising minds this century. You go into a studio with Larry, and you're watching art. It's beautiful." He laughed, then added, "From my standpoint, it's beautiful."

Dukakis told me that the Horton ad took his record wildly out of context. A Republican predecessor had created the Massachusetts furlough program,

> he said, and forty-four states had similar programs at the time, including California; Ronald Reagan had instituted it there when he was governor. Two California parolees committed murders while furloughed. Dukakis said that he blamed himself for not responding more forcefully: "I made a big, big mistake by not attacking back" (p. 42).

At least three lessons from this story are that:

1. You can defeat someone who is in the lead – with one attack ad.
2. You have to play the game – you have to attack back, or you're sunk.
3. Misrepresentation is fine – in fact, it's "beautiful."

Swift Boat Controversy

The next most well-known attack ad, of course, came in 2004, against Democratic presidential candidate John Kerry, a decorated Vietnam war veteran and a Senator for nearly 20 years, at the time of the election. The attack ad was promoted, along with a book, by the "Swift Boat Veterans for Truth." They said he was "unfit to be Commander-in-Chief." Even Republican President Bush and Senator McCain rejected these claims:

> "I think the Bush campaign should specifically condemn the ad," The Associated Press quoted Mr. McCain, Republican of Arizona and a Vietnam War veteran, as saying.

> Mr. Bush's campaign did not do so, but Nicolle Devenish, Mr. Bush's campaign communications director, said, "We have never and will never question John Kerry's service." She did not address the content of the advertisement, from a group of anti-Kerry veterans calling themselves "Swift Boat Veterans for Truth."
>
> Mr. Kerry earned a Bronze Star, a Silver Star and three Purple Hearts commanding a Swift boat in Vietnam.
>
> Swift Boat Veterans for Truth is one of the so-called 527 committees, named for a provision in the tax code that created them. Federal law allows such groups to raise unlimited donations and run advertisements so long as they do not expressly call for the election or defeat of a federal candidate. The Democrats have been far more reliant on such groups than the Republicans this election. …
>
> None of the men served with Mr. Kerry on his Swift boat but claim to have served on boats that were often near his (Rutenberg, 2004).

Apparently, John Kerry did not respond to these attacks during the summer pause before the fall election push that year, which he later sorely regretted. Since then, this case has been cited as the most common example of attack ads:

> Since the 2004 election, the term "Swift Boating" (or "swiftboating") has become a common expression for a campaign attacking opponents by ques-

> tioning their credibility and patriotism. The term is most often used with the pejorative meaning of a smear campaign, but has also been used positively by a neo-conservative.
>
> Wikipedia, 7-25-12:http:en.wikipediaorg-wiki Swift_Vets_and_POWs_for_Truth

But, the Swift Boat ad was not the biggest factor in the election, according to the recent New Yorker article. It was another ad, endorsed by George W. Bush:

> In 2004, McCarthy believed that he had nearly achieved his ambition—the "perfect spot"—with an ad for George W. Bush, called "Ashley's Story." Created for another independent group, the Progress for America Voter Fund, it showed Bush embracing a teen-age girl whose mother had been killed on September 11, 2001, in Al Qaeda's attack on the World Trade Center. The girl, Ashley, looked into the camera and said of Bush, "He's the most powerful man in the world, and all he wants to do is make sure I'm safe." The group bought more than fourteen million dollars' worth of airtime for the ad, much of it in the key swing state of Ohio, where Ashley lived; it was the biggest single ad buy of the 2004 Presidential campaign. Two backers, both California business executives, contributed five million dollars apiece. Bob Shrum, a Democratic operative, was the principal strategist for Bush's opponent, Senator John Kerry, and he blames the ad for the Democrats' defeat. "The ad

was pretty close to decisive in Ohio," Shrum said. "And Ohio was the whole thing."

McCarthy's defenders argue that the Ashley ad proves that he can do powerful positive spots. Alex Castellanos, a Republican media consultant, says, "He's the Deion Sanders of politics. He can play offense or defense." Shrum, however, argues that the Ashley ad was "all about fear. The message was: 'My mother was killed.'" He adds, "Was it skillfully made? Yes. But the exploitation of 9/11 was reprehensible" (Mayer, 2012, p. 47).

Using Little Girls

Just as in family courts, many of the political attack ad battles involve manipulation of the decision-makers with children – especially young girls. In Family Courts, high-conflict parents often want their children to testify against the other parent. "See, my daughter hates her father. Isn't that proof enough that he's a monster and should have no contact – ever!" While quite controversial, judges are interviewing children more these days and new laws are encouraging that.

It is sad that, since the adults cannot seem to resolve these high-conflict cases, the children are being drawn into the battle more and more. Who can resist the sad and persuasive emotions of a child? The problem is that children are survivors and they know that to survive they must generally agree with the more powerful parent, who is often the more disturbed and narcissistic HCP. Such parents care less about the trauma the child is going through and more about "winning."

This dynamic seems to apply directly to politics (note all of the baby-holding and baby-kissing by candidates over the years), and especially to attack ads. Perhaps the most famous ad of all in this industry was the one about Republican Presidential Candidate Barry Goldwater, put out by the Democratic candidate – who won:

> Arguably, no modern ad has matched the overkill of the 1964 "Daisy" ad, created by President Lyndon B. Johnson's campaign. Footage of a freckled little girl, counting the petals she was plucking off a flower, shifted into a doomsday countdown capped by a billowing mushroom cloud; the insinuation was that if Johnson's opponent, Barry Goldwater, won he'd trigger World War Three (Mayer, 2012, p. 41).

Newt Gingrich's Rise and Fall

Newt Gingrich has been one of the most influential conservatives in the Republican Party over the past 20 years. He was significantly responsible for Republicans regaining the House of Representatives in 1994, during Democratic President Bill Clinton's first term. Their success was based significantly on Gingrich's efforts promoting the "Contract with America." This Contract was signed by almost all Republican candidates for the House right before the election, including several specific promises to reduce the federal government, taxes and other conservative goals. But, more about the Contract below, under the heading "Pre-Marital Agreements in Politics."

After his early success in 1994, Gingrich went on to facilitate shutting down the federal government over budget confrontations with President Bill Clinton, who was largely seen to win these conflicts. Gingrich also got into ethical problems over finances as the Speaker of the House, and was driven from office. He remained active on the fringes of Washington, DC, serving as a highly paid consultant and remained active in conservative politics.

At the time of the primary elections in early 2012, Gingrich had been out of office and mostly out of the public eye for several years. Yet conservatives loved him, and he was a Tea Party ally – and the Tea Party seemed to be driving the Republican Party. While he got off to a shaky start, with campaign committee reorganizations and money trouble, he started surging as actual primary elections were being held, especially in the Southern states. While he lost in Iowa, a caucus state, he won Georgia and was appearing to gain momentum heading into Florida. Here's where attack ads come in:

> McCarthy, who is fifty-nine, helps direct the pro-Romney group Restore Our Future, one of the hundreds of new Super PACs – technically independent political-action committees set up by supporters of the candidates – that are dramatically reshaping the Presidential election...
>
> In Florida, Restore Our Future spent $8.7 million on ads, most of which targeted Gingrich, hastening the end of his brief front-runner status in the state. It was a replay of Iowa, where, the previous month, Restore Our Future had helped crush Gingrich's lead by spending three million dollars on negative ads. The theme of the ads, which were made by McCarthy's firm, was Gingrich's "baggage." The cleverest spot employed a visual gag of battered suitcases, plastered with Gingrich bumper stickers, tumbling down an airport luggage car-

rousel. One by one, the bags popped open. A green suitcase exploded with loose dollar bills – ostensibly ill-gotten gains from his work as a consultant to Freddie Mac. Another disgorged a video of Gingrich looking chummy with Nancy Pelosi, a Democrat who is particularly disliked by conservatives. A female narrator, sounding like a stern mom, listed so many transgressions by Gingrich that the ad became a blur of disqualifying scandal, summed up in the final attack line: "Newt Gingrich – too much baggage!"

At least one of the ad's accusations was demonstrably false. As a close-up of a Chinese flag saturated the screen with red, the narrator claimed that Gingrich and Pelosi had "co-sponsored a bill that gave sixty million dollars a year to a U.N. program supporting China's brutal one-child policy." Politifact, the nonpartisan fact-checking organization, assessed the bill in question, the Global Warming Prevention Act of 1989, and found that it barred any U.S. funds from being used to pay for "the performance of involuntary sterilization or abortion or to coerce any person to accept family planning." The claim earned Politifact's lowest rating: Pants on Fire.

A few days after the spot began airing across Iowa, a reporter for the Huffington Post noticed that even residents who said they paid little attention to campaign ads often mentioned one prevailing concern about Gingrich: he had too much baggage. Evidently, McCarthy's message was sticking. Col-

> leagues note that McCarthy is a shrewd consumer of "O," or opposition research, on the rival candidates he's targeting, and that he hones his message using polls, focus groups, micro-targeting data, and "perception analyzers" – meters that evaluate viewers' split-second reactions to demo tapes.
>
> For all the effort that goes into calibrating the scripts, McCarthy's ads often have the crude look of a hastily assembled PowerPoint presentation. They feature hokey graphics – key criticisms are highlighted with neon-yellow stripes – and a heavy-handed use of black-and-white to lend a sinister cast to images. The ads are the political equivalent of a supermarket tabloid, emphasizing the personal and the sensational. But when they hit their mark they are dazzlingly effective (Mayer, 2012, 40-41) (bold added).

This is a good example of the power of Super PACs and their attack ads, even over conservative candidates. Perhaps the Republican Party saw Gingrich as a high-conflict politician, who had risen based on all-or-nothing solutions, personal attacks, and negative emotions; but who had also fallen, much because of the same traits. As we have explained before in the business world, narcissistic leaders often rise dramatically and fall dramatically. Is Newt Gingrich a narcissistic HCP? We're not saying he is or he isn't. But his experience appears instructive in terms of negative advocates – for and against him.

Premarital Agreements in Politics

Today's high-conflict politics is also similar to high-conflict divorce in another surprising way – Pre-Marital Agreements (also known as Prenuptial Agreements). As described above, Newt Gingrich was a driving force behind the Contract with America in 1994, signed by almost all Republican candidates for Congress. On the surface, that seems like a brilliant move – and it worked in the short-term, delivering both the House and the Senate to Republicans.

However, it seemed to run into the problem of some Premarital Agreements in marriages – they risk driving a wedge between the spouses, creating polarization and making it impossible for them to work together toward any common goals. The premarital agreement makes you a potential negative advocate for someone (or something) else outside of the marriage. It's like saying you're still married to someone (or something) else, to whom you owe more loyalty than you ever will to your new spouse. Perhaps you're married to your money, such as the wealthy husband who wants a Premarital Agreement because he does not intend to share any of it with his new lower-income wife, if things do not work out.

When these couples divorce, there is the risk that the premarital agreement will become a source of high-conflict litigation – usually over whether it was properly signed with knowledge of its effects, or was coercive, and the new spouse didn't know what she was getting into. Or, perhaps you're still dealing with your former spouse, to whom you owe money, share children or other issues. If the former spouse is an HCP, then the new spouse often complains about the former spouse dominating the new marriage, and some second marriages can't survive the stress. Other new marriages, however, figure out how to cope with the former spouse without letting it disrupt their own negotiations and happiness.

Of course, it could be argued that the "someone" in politics was the American people who agreed with it – to whom Congress should be loyal. On the other hand, it can be argued that the purpose of Congress is to have our representatives negotiate and make decisions that represent all Americans and their various points of view in the discussions.

In terms of politics, such a contract seems to imply that you will not negotiate in good faith with the other representatives in Congress on many of the most important issues facing the country. It starts the relationship with polarization, and that appears to be what happened in the 1990's. Right away, those who signed the Contract with America were demanding changes, and many of them were adopted. On the other hand, it drove the federal government into a crisis, leading to the balanced budget confrontations between the Republican congress and the Democratic president (Clinton).

Similar crises have been repeated up to the present, with the show-down between Republicans and Democratic President Obama over the debt ceiling in the summer of 2011. Another such show-down will reoccur in 2013, soon after the next election in November (we are writing this in July 2012).

While there hasn't been another Contract with America since 1994, hundreds of Republican congressional candidates have signed a more limited Taxpayer Protection Pledge, developed by Grover Norquist, a conservative adviser and Washington lobbyist. This pledge says that the signer *will never vote to raise taxes.* Norquist is famous for saying that he wanted to shrink the federal budget to be so small that you could "drown it in a bathtub." Are the signers his negative advocates? Is he an HCP? We don't know. He seems to specialize in all-or-nothing solutions. However, in these polarized times, even some Republicans are rebelling against such a premarital-like agreement, for the same reasons that many brides and grooms do:

> Rigell is not the only GOP candidate who has publicly expressed concerns over the anti-tax pledge. Young Gun Richard Tisei's (R-Mass.) campaign circulated a SALEM NEWS article last month declaring that the candidate is "bucking the trend" and will be "one of the lone dissidents" if elected to Congress.
>
> Tisei, running against Rep. John Tierney (D-Mass.), said he has known Norquist since his college days, when Tisei was the chairman of College Republicans at American University and Norquist was the executive director of the national organization. Still, the former Massachusetts state senator insisted he wants to avoid getting "tied up in knots" if he's elected.
>
> "I'm not signing any pledges," Tisei told The Huffington Post last week. "I'm just promising to use my best judgment as a congressman. And I think that's the problem in Washington right now. You have both Democrats and Republicans that are inflexible on certain issues" (Svitek, 2012).

Conclusion

Negative advocates absorb the all-or-nothing solutions, personal attacks and highly negative emotions of high-conflict people, and take them to a higher level. They often appear more credible than the HCP himself or herself, and may be in a better position to repeatedly make negative statements that will become absorbed in others' minds. This seems to be just as true in high-conflict elections as it is in high-conflict divorce.

Yet, the more that people become aware of the role of negative advocates in the splitting dynamic, the more reasonable they tend to become. The judge in the Hollywood divorce found reasonable solutions, rather than getting hooked in by the parties' possibly negative advocates. Some politicians also are learning to resist getting hooked in by all-or-nothing "premarital-like" solutions.

...the more that people become aware of the role of negative advocates in the splitting dynamic, the more reasonable they tend to become.

Unfortunately, both parties and their negative advocates have turned to advertising in a big and disheartening way. As history shows, at times Democrats have been more willing to do this, and at other times Republicans appear more willing. We are concerned about the splitting dynamic from any side that engages in it. It is divisive and will escalate our nation's polarization higher and higher, until it is stopped.

While there seem to be more current examples of Republican Super PAC money and negativity in attack ads, we want to end this chapter emphasizing that both parties are engaged in this behavior, and that it is occurring in national, state and local elections. It doesn't matter whether a candidate is an HCP, a negative advocate, or just trying to cope in a polarized world. This high-conflict behavior is unacceptable for anyone, and, as we will explain in the last chapter, it is unnecessary:

> This is hardly to say that the Democrats have clean hands. One Priorities U.S.A. Action "Mitt Romney's America," earned a "four Pinocchios" rating from the Washington Post. It claimed, dubiously, that Romney would leave "Medicare dismantled" and "Social Security privatized." And critics say that a recent ad made by the Democratic National Committee took an offhand remark by Romney—"I like being able to fire people"—out of context. "Yes, he said it, but he was talking about firing insurance companies that don't do a good job," Mike Murphy, a Republican media consultant, says. He calls such deliberately misleading ads "pejoratively true." Murphy, who used to be known as Murphy the Mudslinger, and once had vanity license plates that read "GO NEG," says that pundits are always lamenting that the current election cycle is the meanest ever. But this time, because of the proliferation of Super PACs, they might be right.
>
> ....
>
> It's not just tougher out there," Hart, the Democratic pollster, says. "It's become a situation where the contest is how much you can destroy the system, rather than how much you can make it work. It makes no difference if you have a 'D' or an 'R' after your name. There's no sense that this is about democracy, and after the election you have

to work together, and knit the country together. The people in the game now just think to the first Tuesday in November, and not a day beyond it" (Mayer, 2012, p. 49) (bold added).

"I need to see another ten or eleven debates before I make up my mind."

Chapter
6

How the News Media Mirror Family Court

Dynamics of Communication

People love to gossip. According to anthropologists, people all over the world gossip, in every tribe, in every village, in every city, and within every country of the world. It serves an important social bonding function for the people in a given community. It functions as a social lubricant to keep conversations going and keep people interacting, so that they can stay aware of each other and watch each other's backs if an enemy or predator is lurking.

Information is power. *First* information about news is even more powerful. Think of the "Breaking News" banner across the CNN broadcasts. Within the news media, the source that gets the news first is top-dog in the industry, and we never stop hearing about it… "You heard this FIRST on…CNN…ABC…NBC…CBS… MSNBC … (fill in the blank)." In ordinary conversations, the person who first gets news can then proudly share it with others, or can hold on to it for a while to build tension. Having control over the news gives one (or a station) a real feeling of power. A lawyer can climax a great trial when she withholds the key witnesses for her side until the end, then explode the courtroom with a dramatic presentation of information that turns the case for them.

With the press promoting conflict and narcissistic high-conflict politicians doing whatever they can to promote themselves, it's no wonder that the world feels more dangerous.

With today's competitive news industry, this love of information and gossip has been taken to a new level. Cable television, major networks and the Internet are all competing for attention, so we have news all day and news all night, in order to capture your attention. This is the result:

> As media outlets multiply and it becomes easier to disseminate information on the Web and on cable, the news cycle is getting shorter—to the point that there is no pause, only the constancy of the Web and the endless argument of cable. This creates pressure to entertain or perish, which has fed the press' dominant bias: not pro-liberal or pro-conservative, but pro-conflict (Auletta, 2010, p. 38) (bold added for emphasis).

With the press promoting conflict and narcissistic high-conflict politicians doing whatever they can to promote themselves, it's no wonder that the world feels more dangerous. This brings us back to the fundamental questions, or two mantras of our age: *Is this really a crisis? Is this really a hero?*

The Impact of Social Media

A great debate is raging in our society over whether the increasing uses of social media, the Internet, and electronic gadgets is increasing or decreasing communication among people today. The most accurate answer is *both* are true; it is increasing and decreasing communication and connectedness among people. However, the form of it has changed dramatically, as we have moved from face-to-face contact with one another to telegraphic communications over the airwaves, via Twitter, emails, Facebook, etc.

While communication is now expected to be instant, some theorists are saying that young people of the current generation are losing their social skills, their ability to read facial expressions, tone of voice, and body language of others, and are missing the more subtle meanings of texted communications.

The problem with all of this is the fact that about 70% of the meaning of communications comes from the non-verbal aspects (gestures, body language, and tone of voice) and only about 30% comes from the actual words said. And, studies with young children demonstrate that, in understanding the communications of others, they first pay attention to the tone (the vocal channel of communication), then to the body language (the visual channel), and only last to the actual words (the verbal channel). We are increasingly limiting our communications to just the words (the weakest aspect of interpersonal communication).

Lack of Contact Breeds Fear, and Fear Breeds Hatred

In addition to just the sheer difficulty of understanding nuanced communications when the vocal and visual channels of communication are missing, when people are in conflict, they tend to avoid direct contact with each other. Many people in a high-conflict divorce process do not communicate directly with one another, if even at all. This significantly reduces the accuracy of the meanings of their communications with each other, because of the absence of the most important cues (the visual and vocal). Instead, they are often reduced to texting or emails, which can feel abrupt, rude, and vague in the accuracy of the intended meaning. And, in higher conflict divorces, there is often a court-order for no contact between the parties.

What we know about the absence of contact between people who need to be in contact is that it breeds suspicion, paranoia, and mistrust.

What we know about the absence of contact between people who need to be in contact is that it breeds suspicion, paranoia, and mistrust. For example, research has shown how there is a connection between the amount of contact that two racial groups have with one another and the degree of racial prejudice and fear between them; the more contact they have with one another, the more positive and trusting they feel about each other, and the absence of effective contact generates fear, and ultimately, hatred. Anger and hatred are powerful feelings, while fear is a weak and vulnerable feeling. So, the anger behind hatred serves to protect us against the vulnerable feeling of fear.

Factoids

When people are really angry in a conflict with another party and they are in the mode of accusing the other side of horrible things and wrong-doings, they regularly assert *factoids*, which are questionable, unverified, false or fabricated statements or half-truths presented as a fact, but with no veracity. More specifically, a factoid is defined by the Compact Oxford English Dictionary as "an item of unreliable information that is repeated so often that it becomes accepted as fact." In both family court cases and the news media, factoids are blathered about constantly.

The re-writing of marital and spousal history that takes place in high-conflict divorce cases (that was described in Chapter 2) is encouraged by each spouse's lawyer, as they file document after document declaring the other as having regularly and repeatedly committed minor to unspeakable offenses, mostly with little evidence other than gossip and factoids as evidence. The operating tactic (in both high-conflict divorce and in high-conflict politics) is to assert, over and over to their listening audience, slanderous comments about the opposing party.

Repetition of such assertions eventually makes them sink into the mind as truths; if said enough times, they start to feel true. This, in fact, is the main strategy that product marketers utilize. Just witness the mindless repetition of commercials on TV, which must be working, because it continues 24/7. Moreover, factoids gain even more credibility when associated with the commonly repeated phrase, "As Seen On TV." If you repeat an assertion enough times on TV, then the phrase "As Seen On TV" gains validity, in a fashion of circular logic, as sort of a self-fulfilling prophecy.

Similarly, a negative attribute can be set up in the same way as a positive one. Decades of persuasion research in social psychology has shown the power of factoids for establishing the appearance of the credibility or incredibility of an assertion, whether it be about an ex-spouse, a commercial product, or a candidate's failings.

With today's electronic means for repeating information, the news media has become the amplifier or megaphone for the messages of narcissistic high-conflict politicians. This is similar to how family courts allow you to keep coming back to air one grievance after another, including personal attacks on the other party, crisis emotions and all-or-nothing solutions. The more you say it, the more it seems to become true. Thus, the courts and the media are perfect fits for spreading high conflict messages by HCPs.

Cognitive Dissonance

A late, famous psychologist, Leon Festinger, developed and researched a theory that asserts when a person has two beliefs that are in contradiction with one another, dissonance is created; the person has to resolve this dissonance by choosing one of the beliefs and supporting it vigorously, while defending it against all reasonable arguments from the other side. So, if a chronic smoker comes to learn that smoking is strongly associated with the development of lung cancer, the person is in a state of dissonance. If the person wants to continue smoking, he must either deny the scientific evidence of its association with lung cancer, or, he must give up smoking.

Often, the person develops strong rationalizations against the scientific evidence, saying to himself such things as: "Scientific conclusions can't be trusted, since they always get reversed over time," or "You don't get cancer for 20 years, so I can still enjoy smoking for a long while," or, "There is no lung cancer in my family history, so those results don't apply to me."

Believing is Seeing

Social Psychologist Elliot Aronson, a student of Leon Festinger, spent his long professional career researching cognitive dissonance. He found its occurrence in a wide variety of settings and concluded that it was a very common dilemma that people regularly had to deal with. When a person finally resolves the dissonance of two competing beliefs, or a belief that is in contradiction with one's actions, from then on the person only allows herself to see what she already believes, as she screens out any competing information.

With today's electronic means for repeating information, the news media has become the amplifier or megaphone for the messages of narcissistic high-conflict politicians.

Carol Tavris & Elliot Aronson (2007) used the expression "Believing is Seeing" as a twist on the more common expression with the reversed wording. This idea is the core basis for the polarization effect by the news media. The media has polarized into the Progressive stations (e.g. MSNBC) and the Conservative stations (e.g. FOX News), with each presenting only one side of any political story and regularly and persistently demeaning the other side, and it is very, very difficult and rare for a person to change their point of view once they have resolved the dissonance in favor of one view. Moreover, by its methods, effective

contact between the polarized groups are minimized, and when a debate is set up, it is, indeed, a set-up; the goal is to fuel high levels of conflict, creating a Romanesque gladiator spectator sport, which makes for better press and generates more viewers.

Edward R. Murrow, the late famous TV anchor and news journalist used to present slow, thoughtful, reasoned analysis of both sides of any dispute, with a focus on coming up with solutions to society's problems. The discussants on his program treated each courteously and with respect and restraint. They presented their ideas with a modicum of etiquette, a quality grossly missing in today's high-conflict news reporting.

The campaigns and debates between candidates for president were largely respectful discussions of the issues. Personal attacks were largely absent, but when one candidate did attack the other candidate, it was done with eloquence, subtlety, and clever innuendo, as compared to the brashness and sledgehammer approach of political attacks today. The candidates were encouraged by the news media to present what they stood for, rather than how awful the other candidate was.

Point-Counterpoint

The TV news of today is probably best captured by the parody portrayed on Saturday Night Live when Dan Aykroyd and Jane Curtin performed "Weekend Update---Point Counter-Point." Jane would stridently present her polarized position on a very controversial topic while verbally assailing Dan with harsh attacks on his character and his intelligence. Dan would then present his "counterpoint" position starting with the now classic phrase, "Jane, you ignorant slut!..." After Dan was finished blasting Jane for her stupidity and immorality, Jane would begin her reply to his reply with the phrase, "Dan, you pompous ass…" And the war of wicked words would whirl on.

On the surface, this is hilarious comedy. However, good comedy is right on the line between fantasy and reality, and it seems that the line has, to our detriment, moved quite a bit towards reality. Today's family court and today's news media both share this trend towards encouraging polarization, conflict, and non-cooperation by its very structure and process.

The Fairness Doctrine

The skit by Aykroyd and Curtin was funny in the 1970s because of the "Fairness Doctrine" in existence at the time. This was a federal government policy established in the 1920s, revoked in 1987, and totally eliminated in 2011. It had the following purposes and short history:

> [It] required that TV and radio stations holding FCC-issued broadcast licenses to (a) devote some of their programming to controversial issues of public importance and (b) allow the airing of opposing views on those issues. This meant that programs on politics were required to include opposing opinions on the topic under discussion. Broadcasters had an active duty to determine the spectrum of views on a given issue and include those people best suited to representing those views in their programming.
>
> Additionally, the rule mandated that broadcasters alert anyone subject to a personal attack in their programming

> and give them a chance to respond, and required any broadcasters who endorse political candidates to invite other candidates to respond.
>
> ....
>
> [After a First Amendment case before the U.S. Supreme Court in 1969] the FCC began to reconsider the rule in the mid-80s, and ultimately revoked it in 1987, after Congress passed a resolution instructing the commission to study the issue. The decision has been credited with the explosion of conservative talk radio in the late '80s and early '90s. While the FCC has not enforced the rule in nearly a quarter century, it remains technically on the books. As a part of the Obama administration's broader efforts to overhaul federal regulation, the FCC is finally scrapping the rule once and for all [in 2011] (Matthews, 2011).

It is interesting to note the timing of these First Amendment changes and their impact on today's political atmosphere. With the *Citizen's United* decision in 2012 by the U.S. Supreme Court and the "final scrapping" of the fairness doctrine, the restraints on high-conflict behavior have been removed in politics. The situation we are in today didn't just happen because people changed, although there are studies suggesting that there are more people with narcissistic personality disorder than forty years ago (Twenge and Campbell, 2009).

The removal of these fairness restraints appears to have had a bigger impact, because it allowed such high-conflict people to rise to the top of politics, with their drive for self-promotion, personal attacks, crisis emotions and all-or-nothing solutions. While removing these restraints may have been well-intentioned, they may have gone too far – especially given the increase in high-conflict people. This is similar to what we see in family courts, with narcissistic high-conflict people dominating this adversarial process and getting the most attention.

Disclaimer About Family Court: While family courts have increasingly supported alternate methods of dispute resolution (such as mediation or collaborative divorce practices), the default method is still the adversarial model of litigation, especially for high-conflict divorces, in which the parties typically are not able to resolve their differences in other ways, so they wind up in litigation. Sadly, they don't resolve their differences in litigation either, but this reality does not deter them from repeatedly trying anyway.

Super negative advocates in divorce and Super PACs in politics are pretty much guaranteed to keep the funding coming, as long as their passions continue to swell for blood in the fight – and the system continues to support it!

Increasing numbers of divorcing couples represent themselves and do not hire attorneys (because of their prohibitive costs or because the particular couples, luckily, neither have nor want a high-conflict divorce). However, the couples in high-conflict divorces typically *must* hire attorneys and pay for it whatever way they can, including borrowing from their respective negative advocates within their tribal warfare clans. As in politics and in divorce, when one runs out of money, it is really hard to keep the brutal battles going.

Fighting, whether in a campaign to be viewed as the best parent, or in a campaign to be viewed as the best candidate, is expensive, both monetarily and emotionally. However, Super negative advocates in divorce and Super PACS in politics are pretty much guaranteed to keep the funding coming, as long as their passions continue to swell for blood in the fight—and the system continues to support it!

How Does Family Court Contribute to High Conflict?

As with candidates running for president, divorce, traditionally, has been viewed as a battle over resources; candidates battle over power, money and voters, in the news media, and high-conflict divorcing couples battle over power, money, and time with children in the family court. Both campaigns are set up in an adversarial climate, and share similar underlying dynamics. Both see their disputes as battles to be won, rather than as mutual problems to be solved.

However, much of how family court contributes to high conflict has to do with the very nature of its structure. When you and your spouse are present in family court, you are instructed to sit far away from each other, at opposite ends of tables, with the lawyers in between you and your soon-to-be ex-. You are not allowed to talk with each other in court, but instead, your lawyers address the judge. On those rare occasions when you are asked a question, you must talk directly to the judge, not to the other party. Remember the research about how the lack of contact between two parties that need to communicate increases feelings of mistrust, fear, and hatred?

Unlike in criminal court, where the evidence presented is tangible (blood stains, DNA, accounting sheets, etc.), the bulk of the evidence presented in family court are feelings, and those feelings typically are intense and extreme. This includes the "feelings" and impressions of all the witnesses (negative advocates) presented in court.

To keep some semblance of control over the court proceedings, the judge requires attorneys to speak for their clients. But, while filtering their clients' feelings, some attorneys have a way of exaggerating the intensity of extreme feelings in such ways as to demean, shame, and invalidate the opposing spouse's humanity.

Of particular concern with very high-conflict divorce cases is the way that the court's structure supports the airing of the high-conflict behavior, regardless of its unreasonableness. Everything said, by the parties, the attorneys and the witnesses (negative advocates) during a court hearing not only is open to the public to hear, but is available to the children of the parties to read, in the years to come (Comparable to the "Free Speech" doctrine in the News Media).

This means that all the horrible things that each of the children's parents (or presidential candidates) said about each other is available for the children (or American public) to read at the age of majority (or whenever they can turn on the TV news). The traumatic experience of a child hearing dreadful and atrocious allegations said by one of his parents against the other is well-documented in the divorce research. And, to think that the family court system is set up for exactly this sort of thing to happen is very problematic. In many cases of high-conflict divorce, the fight over the extra day of visitation pales in comparison to the damage done to the child in learning of the degrading things said by his parents about each other.

Moreover, the system is set up for lawyers to have financial incentives to keep the conflict going. By continuing to defend their high-conflict client, assert horrible and demeaning things about the other parent, and obstruct and prevent a resolution to the conflict, they stand to make a lot of money (some call it "churning"). In other arenas of society, this would be considered unethical and perhaps even slanderous behavior. But, in the field of law, it is considered upholding the canons of one's legal obligation, which is to "zealously advocate" for your client.

The problem with applying this same method to high-conflict child custody cases is that doing so encourages parents to polarize, prove and publicly air how bad the other parent is, and battle over who is the better parent. And, everything we know from research of children of divorce is that the inter-parental fight is the thing that destroys the well-being of the child. In essence, then, the court's very structure is set up to accomplish exactly the opposite of what we know allows children to emotionally survive divorce, by its allowance and encouragement of the public displays of anger, conflict, and hatred, and discouraging a forum for conflict resolution and compromise. One could not design a better structure for destroying children whose parents are going through divorce.

Does any of this sound similar to the news media, with TV, radio, and the Internet allowing and encouraging all opinions to be aired, and high-conflict opinions to be aired first? Is it really helpful for American voters to hear awful, scathing things (including many factoids) about their future or current president? Does it really add to your trust in your candidates' credibility to hear such high-conflict rhetoric just because it makes money or increases viewership for the media?

Here is a comparative summary of the strategies used by the news media and family court that perpetuate polarization:

Strategies in the News Media	Strategies in Family Court
1. The goal of polarized news reporting is to establish an extreme position about a candidate.	1. The goal of the family court structure is to encourage the airing of two extreme positions about the needs of a child after parental separation and the financial needs of the parents.
2. The goal of gaining real power of information is achieved by being the first to report a news item.	2. The goal of gaining real power of information is achieved by being the first to aggressively slam the other parent's faults and weaknesses.
3. The asserting of factoids (regardless of the facts) begins to set a particular extreme point of view into the minds of the audience.	3. The asserting of intense negative feelings and factoids (regardless of the facts) about the other parent is designed to set a particular extreme point of view into the mind of the judge.
4. The repetition of these factoids is aimed at establishing credibility of the point of view.	4. The repetition of these factoids (by the lawyers and the witnesses / negative advocates) is aimed at establishing credibility of a particular side's point of view.
5. Cognitive dissonance is resolved by only listening to what one already believes.	5. Cognitive dissonance is set up by the attorneys (through the presentation of contradictory evidence) to destroy the credibility (and goodness) of the other parent and to get the judge to resolve her dissonance in favor of one party.
6. Thus, the polarization process of all good and all evil is solidly established, with little likelihood of a change of mind.	6. Thus, the polarization process of one all-good parent and one all-evil parent is solidly established, with little likelihood of a judge's change of mind.

"We used to feel your pain, but that's no longer our policy."

Chapter
7

A Nation of Alienated Voters and Alienated Children

It has been well noted by journalists and sociologists that large numbers of today's voters feel alienated by our current high-conflict political process. However, as an individual voter, you actually might respond to this situation in any of several different ways. We see strong parallels between the major ways that children cope with high-conflict divorces and the way voters cope with high-conflict politics, and it is just these very dynamics that seem to be pulling us as a nation into very serious dysfunction. Let us explore these parallels, first with the child from divorce, followed by the voter from a split nation, for each scenario.

When you are a child with parents in a high-conflict divorce, and your parents relentlessly attack each other, show no inkling of cooperation with one another, and regularly put you and your siblings in the middle of their disputes, you are faced with several available options:

1. You can repeatedly try to stop your parents from fighting (typically a futile action);

2. You can join with and take on the side of one of your parents in the battle;

3. You can "leave the field", detach from both parents, and not allow yourself to get caught up in the battle.

(Note: Because of a wide range of individual differences, temperaments, tolerances, and sensitivities among the different children in a given family, each child may wind up selecting a different option than those selected by his or her sibling).

In the **first** high-conflict divorce scenario, you wind up feeling frustrated, powerless, and hopeless. You feel that, as your parents continue their endless fighting, they are not there for you and, if a critical situation were to arise in which you really need them, they would just continue to focus on their fight with each other and not at all on you. They are so preoccupied with themselves that they have no left over energy or capacity to focus on you and your needs, and as such, they are unable to raise you properly.

You feel abandoned, you feel very sad, and you feel very angry. You begin to figure out ways to take care of your own emotional needs. You scold and yell at your parents to stop fighting. You try to get other people to jolt your parent out of their madness. You may even resort to creating a very big problem (e.g. getting in fights at school; flunking out of school; becoming suicidal; shooting someone; setting the house on fire), hoping your parents will join together to solve your problem, perhaps in therapy sessions with a sane adult present!

These are actual ways that some children use in their attempts to deal with their warring parents; ways that are sometimes motivated consciously and sometimes unconsciously.

Political Parallel to First Scenario

You might continue to vote, but you actively continue to try to make the political system work, against formidable odds.

Motivated by feelings of sadness and frustration about the polarized, conflicted political system, you write letters to your congressional representatives, send letters to the editors of news publications, participate as an activist in public protests, and actively plead to each presidential candidate to work together with the other side. Even against much frustration, you continue trying to get the opposing candidates to resolve their differences and get their work done. You might call in to talk-radio shows and rant about how unreasonably both candidates are acting, and maybe even offer solutions, from solid to outrageous.

You experience much personal stress over the political issues, which can affect your own physical and mental health and your personal relationships. You rant about the polarized issues of gun control, abortion, and healthcare, and you worry about your own and your family's safety, health, and well-being, believing that if you just keep voicing your concerns, the political candidates will eventually listen to reason, stop fighting with one another, come to their senses and solve the nation's many pressing problems.

The **second** high-conflict divorce scenario involves a more psychologically complex dynamic and is utilized by those who cannot tolerate the constant feeling of powerless as they try to stop their parents' fighting. In this scenario, you attempt to deal with the on-going parental feud by aligning (mostly an unconscious process) with one parent against the other in order to resolve your cognitive dissonance (i.e. "I love *both* my parents, but my parents will not let me love them both, so I must align with one parent and begin to avoid and hate the other parent, just like my newly preferred parent does."). Psychologically, this resolution allows the child to at least not lose *both* parents (a terrifying position, especially for younger children). However, the child *is* left with losing one of her parents.

Nothing that the opposing candidate (or any other candidate of that political party) could ever do would be viewed positively—they are terminally and certifiably vilified.

As discussed in Chapter Two, this is the model that was previously called "Parental Alienation Syndrome" and is now called "The Alienated Child." To reiterate, it is characterized by a child putting down and refusing all contact with one parent, as the child resists and rejects all visitation and communication with that parent, even to the point of running away or suicide if forced to see that parent.

Over time, the supportive parent escalates the conflict and begins to level charges (of child molest, physical abuse, parental neglect, and worse) against the maligned parent – mostly based upon no credible evidence. As a child in this type of alienation, you are swept up in a maelstrom of allegations by one parent against the other, in which you actively participate and to which you may actively contribute. Your maligned parent usually has to fight back and counter-accuse the maligning parent of "poisoning the well," which, in the fashion of a self-fulfilling prophecy, simply gives more fodder to the child and maligning parent of "how mean he really is and how much gall he has that he would accuse the 'good' parent of *anything*."

As long as you maintain your "split" position of having one all-good parent and one all-bad parent, you feel secure that you will at least keep a solid relationship with one of your parents through this war. However, if ever you consider something even remotely positive about the other parent, you risk your preferred parent no longer loving you. This is an all-or-none game! There is no middle choice. The name of the game is POLARIZATION, and your emotional and psychological survival is at stake!

Political Parallel to Second Scenario

You might continue to vote but pick one candidate's side or one party's side and join in the party-line on every issue and criticize but no longer listen to the rhetoric of the other side.

You might be among the voters that choose one political side on all issues. You assume the "identity" of a Republican or of a Democrat and lash out against the other side on every issue available, making the opposing candidate wrong, bad, evil, and corrupt. Nothing that the opposing candidate (or any other candidate of that political party) could ever do would be viewed positively – they are terminally and certifiably vilified. You might spend all your time, energy, and money supporting and polarizing your candidate against the other side. You vote the party line on every election.

In this strategy of coping with non-stop high-conflict politics, you become incensed and outraged whenever a friend or family member suggests anything positive about the opposing candidate, or his or her positions on any issue. This is now a personal thing, not just a friendly conversation about issues.

You sometimes have lost friendships, permanently alienated family members over these issues, or locked yourself out of being able to engage in certain topics of conversations with your family or friends (i.e. anything political). You simply cannot tolerate hearing the other's point of view on anything political. It feels as though your very existence is at stake at the mere thought of compromising your beliefs or even thinking compassionately about the other side.

If you are a staunch Democrat using this coping strategy, listening to Rush Limbaugh would be akin to being forced to agree with Hitler! If you are a staunch Republican using this coping strategy, watching Jon Stewart would cause feelings of revulsion and nausea and make you feel that you have just been poisoned! These are all very visceral feelings of hatred that become so hard-wired into your belief system, that you quickly resolve any cognitive dissonance that may arise by banishing the views of the "enemy" from your attention and your mind ("Not Seeing is Not Believing").

You develop a morbid fear of being "tainted" and "contaminated" by the awful, toxic, evil ideas of the other side; as if you might, against your will, get pulled over to the "Dark Side." This feeling is intensely similar to that of a child who has been effectively alienated from one parent by the other parent and his or her tribal divorce system, i.e. the negative advocates.

In the **third** high-conflict divorce scenario, a child comes to recognize the utter futility of playing their parents' "game." One adult who had grown up all her life within a high-conflict, never-ending divorce dynamic of her parents, sadly said:

> *When I was just four years old, I realized that my parents had nothing to offer me…their lives were organized completely around the on-going battle with each other. I had to find my own way to grow up on my own. I have always just thought of my parents as nuts, and I've never had any respect for either of them… they were just totally self-absorbed, self-centered, and selfish.*

When you have selected this third option, you learn, sometimes very early on in life, that you cannot count on your parents to protect or nurture you – you hear shouted inside your head: THEY HATE EACH OTHER MORE THAN THEY LOVE YOU! You must detach from them for your survival, and even when you do that, your survival is at stake if you cannot get someone else to help you grow up.

You may not survive if you can't figure out on your own how to navigate the many scary situations that you'll face in life, without solid parental guidance. You have a feeling that is deeper and more profound than the sadness experienced by the child in the first scenario – that child is still in the game and, in spite of the frustrations, somewhere still has hope that the war might end ("…If only I try hard enough, or have enough problems with which to distract them and bring them together.").

You're facing an existential dilemma caused by the lack of solid and consistent guidance about how to live. When your mother tells you one thing and your father tells you the opposite, you don't know who to believe. In fact, because younger children (and many adults) do not have the capacity to maintain two contradictory realities and do believe that there can only be one truth, they conclude that one of their parents is lying to them; the problem is they don't know which parent is lying, so, they come to not believe either parent. They lose trust that their parents will tell them the truth – about anything! When you don't have a parent on whom you can count to tell you the truth, who can you believe?

The term "anomie" seems apt here.

The Merriam-Webster Dictionary defines "anomie" as: *"Social instability resulting from a breakdown of standards and values; personal unrest, alienation, and anxiety that comes from a lack of purpose or ideals."*

Indeed, that is what you feel if you have detached from your parents' fight as a way to cope. You feel uprooted, alienated, anxious and lost in the world. Without the trusted guidance of your parents (when both are in agreement and cooperating with each other), you don't know what to do. You don't know what is right, what is good, what is true, what to believe in, who to count on, or who to trust. You are truly an alienated person experiencing anomie, with few or no values, few or no built-in rules of conduct, little sense of self-regulation, and little sense of purpose. The seeds of depression and self-destructive behaviors run deep with this coping strategy.

Political Parallel to Third Scenario

You might stop voting and detach yourself from the political process entirely.

Last, you might be among the voters that choose to no longer vote in any elections and feel it is fruitless to vote. You might believe and say things like, "It doesn't really matter if you vote or not… our elected officials are just going to continue to fight with each other and be ineffective and inept at getting anything done."

You might feel that the limited options available in our seriously polarized two-party system make it impossible to develop a reasonable and workable compromised position on any important issue. You might feel that voting for an independent candidate that might actually make sense is a wasted vote, since the two dominant parties always have the election all sewn up (as a result of the enormous amounts of money that they garner, largely from the Super Pacs).

Take a news fast.

You may feel so hopeless that you detach from the political process, as a way to cope with the overwhelming feeling of powerlessness. You may feel that the system is way too big, too cumbersome, too intimidating, and too intense for you to participate comfortably.

Temperamentally, you may be too sensitive to even expose yourself to the high-conflict rhetoric spewed daily and nightly in the news media by the candidates and their negative advocates. You may find that even listening to a news media presentation of the most neutral assessment of the issues feels like a re-stimulation of earlier trauma when you've listened to the countless other high-conflict discussions on the issues.

A number of years ago, when high-conflict politics was on the rise, health guru Andrew Weil encouraged stressed people to "take a news fast" just one day a week to start, then each week to increase the number of days by one until you no longer watch or listen to the news at all. In making such a recommendation, he was noting the research showing that a major contributor to stress in many people was witnessing the daily news.

Not only are the horrible crimes of murder, rape, drug and alcohol abuse and child abuse featured, but as the candidates argue with each other over who is going to solve those problems better (i.e. over who is the better parent for the nation), neither of them ever seems to solve any of these problems, no matter how many elections take place (remember our mantra: "Is he really a hero?"). This leads viewers to witness ghastly problems but experience no power to create solutions.

Social science research has well-documented an interesting finding about the feeling of powerlessness. They find a direct correlation between seeing the successful end product of your work and your feelings of power and control. In large factories, the people who work on assembly lines and only ever see their one fender that they place repetitively on the chassis of the cars on the assembly line, but never see the finished car, feel the strongest sense of powerlessness. Eventually, many feel depression and a lack of purpose (anomie).

The American voters have been increasingly subjected to a high-conflict, polarized political dynamic that has caused a large portion of the population to become alienated and powerless. We have high intensity, 24/7 news that continuously reports on high intensity events that are debated by high intensity political candidates, pundits, negative advocates, and the likes. In spite of all that talk, they never seem to actualize solutions, but merely continue to magnify the problems within a high-conflict climate. It is no wonder that Andrew Weil gave such sensible advice to turn off the news to reduce stress. However, for most voters who listen to the high-conflict politics, the options for effective responses appear to be seriously limited – the exact feeling experienced by children from high-conflict divorce!

"In Washington today, the sun rose over Capitol Hill and received broad bipartisan support."

Chapter
8

Healing a Split Nation

Throughout this book, we have made an effort to be neutral and to respect the natural differences between Democrats and Republicans, and liberals and conservatives. We believe that the country needs both, and even more points of view.

We both are family mediators and recognize the success that families can have in dealing with very difficult and very personal issues – by listening well, respecting each other's points of view, and avoiding turning "issues" into personal attacks. Surely, politicians should be able to do this, as well.

The splitting dynamic is highly destructive to families – and to nations. It turns peace into war, unnecessarily. In most high-conflict divorces, this dynamic appears to be driven by high-conflict individuals with borderline or narcissistic personality traits.

In politics, the splitting dynamic appears to be driven by narcissistic HCPs and their negative advocates who are driving a wedge into the heart of America. While this book was written before the 2012 presidential election, we believe its concerns will apply for many years into the future.

In politics, the splitting dynamic appears to be driven by narcissistic HCPs and their negative advocates who are driving a wedge into the heart of America.

High-conflict behavior is very present in state and local elections, as well. If it continues to mirror high-conflict divorce, then this behavior will continue to rage on between elections – as though they never really happened – and campaigns will be endless and increasingly like tribal warfare.

Relationship Conflict Resolution

As we stated earlier in this book, there are two types of conflict resolution. One type is purely adversarial and isn't concerned with future relationships; courts operate within this model, as do armies in wartime. The goal is to eliminate the opposition and to prevail. The second type is more cooperative and collaborative and has as its goal to preserve an on-going relationship for the future, beyond the particular dispute that brings the parties together.

In sports and in political elections (at least until recently), there has been the realization that the game is more important than the winner of any particular contest. Winners will lose sometimes, and losers will win sometimes. Good sportsmanship often involves shaking hands and giving credit to the other's good playing and teamwork, regardless of who won.

Marriages and divorces ought to be like this, too, especially when children are involved. You can't destroy the other parent and then send the children over to his or her house and expect the child to feel safe, and to thrive and flourish, emotionally. However, over the past years we have seen a dramatic increase in high-conflict divorces where acceptance of the shared parenting relationship has diminished. Many high-conflict parents believe that the goal is to destroy or eliminate the other parent.

But, eliminating the other parent has not been the goal of the courts, or an option in most cases. Even today, when a parent is found to have been abusive to a child or a spouse, courts still make strong efforts to keep that parent involved with the child – even if it requires professional supervision, or is for very restricted periods of time.

Over the past decade or so, we know of many high-conflict cases in which the lawyers, and sometimes even the mental health professionals, have grown to hate those on the "other side." Domestic violence, child sexual abuse, and parental alienation are some of the "issues" that appear to have contributed to this effect. But, in the majority of high-conflict cases, the facts are often exaggerated, minimized or completely wrong.

When there is clear-cut abuse, the focus is on what to do, and the results often include serious efforts for one or both parties to change their own behavior. The goal is to teach and require positive parenting behavior, which includes learning effective *relationship* conflict resolution skills. Relationships matter, especially to children. But in high-conflict cases, the battle rages over the most basic facts and interpretations of facts as to what happened even yesterday in court! With rampant disrespect and a total lack of self-restraint, HCPs and their negative advocates will never stop.

A Balanced Approach to Politics

Today's high-conflict politicians (and those reasonable politicians who are mirroring high-conflict behavior) seem to have forgotten the importance of relationships.

The Senate seems to be mirroring this shift from past collaborative relationship-building to an adversarial stance with regard to relationships. It wasn't so adversarial until fairly recently:

> When Alexis de Tocqueville visited the Senate, in 1832, he was deeply impressed by the quality of its members: "They represent only the lofty thoughts [of the nation] and the generous instincts animating it, not the petty passions." But he also recognized that "a minority of the nation dominating the Senate could completely paralyze the will of the majority represented in the other house, and that is contrary to the spirit of constitutional government." As long as the Senate continued to be composed of America's most talented statesmen, Tocqueville implied, it would restrain its own anti-democratic potential (Packer, 2010).

This lack of relationships between the parties in the Senate coincides directly with the overall lack of self-restraint. As de Tocqueville suggested, without a concern for relationships with others in the nation, a minority can paralyze the majority if it wants to – and self-restraint seems in short supply among today's narcissistic high-conflict politicians.

If you believe that you, exclusively, hold all the right answers, why even deal with the "other side?" Certainly, this relationship-ignoring approach has been a failure when it comes to co-parenting after divorce. Conflict just keeps escalating, because no one is eager to be a loser in a relationship in which only one person can be right.

Mental Health Treatment for Splitting

The treatment for splitting is to establish balance and integration. This has been well-researched in the field of mental health and has been applied for years in business, as we will show below. Borderline personality disorder, which is reported as affecting approximately 6% of the general population, is particularly known as a disorder in which splitting is common. One of the most effective treatments has been developed by Marsha Linehan, Ph. D., a psychologist with the University of Washington in Seattle. At the core of this method, called Dialectical Behavior Therapy or "DBT," there is an emphasis on counseling clients to recognize and integrate the opposite poles that seem to exist throughout their lives.

This method teaches clients to "integrate the opposites," by recognizing that both sides of a problem may be true.

This method teaches clients to "integrate the opposites," by recognizing that both sides of a problem may be true. For example, you can be a good person AND learn new skills. This is especially important, because so many people with disorders think that they must be all right as is, or terribly flawed if others expect them to learn something new. They have great difficulty accepting themselves.

By teaching themselves how to integrate the opposite ideas about themselves – and others – they can gradually learn skills to manage their own behavior and perceptions of the world. The success of such methods was recently reported in Time Magazine (Cloud, 2009) as showing success in most patients within a year. According to a study at Harvard called the McLean Study of Adult Development mentioned in the Time article, 88% of those who received this or similar treatment were able to overcome or manage this disorder and no longer be diagnosed with BPD ten years later.

While high-conflict politicians tend to have more traits of narcissistic personality disorder than of borderline personality disorder, in terms of the splitting dynamic, the problem is the same: seeing one side as evil and the other side as perfect. Perhaps we should put all of the members of Congress in group therapy and see if DBT would work on them!

Polarity Management

In the 1970's, Barry Johnson, Ph.D., developed a business conflict resolution method called "Polarity Management." Since then, he has conducted a wide range of corporate training and management consulting. His approach has been particularly useful in handling change in large businesses, and in diversity training by helping people of diverse backgrounds get along at work. He has also applied it to polarities in faith-based communities.

His method promotes an approach which can (and should) be applied to situations like splitting in today's politics. The basic idea of Polarity Management is that many conflicts are not problems to "solve," but polarities to "manage," without trying to eliminate one pole or the other. He describes the difference (Johnson, 1992; 1996) by asking two key questions about any conflict:

1. **Is the difficulty ongoing?**

   Problems to solve have a solution which can be con idered an end point in a process, i.e. they are solvable.

   Polarities to manage, on the other hand, do not get "solved." They are ongoing. We are always in the ongoing process of "solving" them, if you will. But they do not have a clear, end point solution. There is a never-ending shift in emphasis or focus from one pole to the other and back. Instead of saying there are problems you actually solve and some that you are continually in a process of solving, I have chosen to call the ongoing process "managing."

2. **Are there two poles which are interdependent?**

   The solution in problems to solve can stand alone. Unlike a polarity to be managed, the solution to a **problem to solve** does not have the necessary opposite that is required for the solution to work over an extended period of time.

> **Polarities to manage**, on the other hand, require a shift in emphasis between opposites such that neither can stand alone. It is a "both/and" difficulty. Both one pole and its apparent opposite depend on each other. The pair are involved in an ongoing, balancing process over an extended period of time. They are interdependent. They need each other.
>
> Johnson, Barry. *Polarity Management: Identifying and Managing Unsolvable Problems.* HRD Press, Amherst, Massachusetts (1992, 1996), p. 82 (bold in original).

Johnson goes on to explain that each pole has an "upside" and a "downside." He predicts exactly the kinds of problems we have when one political group or party gets too much power over another. Each side is blind to its own "downside" and to the other's "upside," so it doesn't seek cooperation and balance, but instead, dominance and elimination of the other. The polarities need to be managed, not resolved in the long-term favor of one group or the other.

The polarities need to be managed, not resolved in the long-term favor of one group or the other.

How would this apply to Democrats and Republicans? Each tries very hard to control all three branches of the federal government: the Presidency, Congress (both the House and the Senate), and the Supreme Court. Yet, whenever this has happened, it has soon created a downside that has driven the other party to finally overcome the imbalance and prevail. This cycle will repeat itself *endlessly*, unless and until both sides see the benefits of working together – then we will have periods of much more stability.

This is similar to certain situations in high-conflict divorce, when, for example, one parent is trying to eliminate the other parent.

And, there are also some advocacy groups for both mothers and for fathers that seem to take this approach. For mothers, there have been victims' advocates against domestic violence and against child abuse. This is a good thing and has brought protection and progress to safer and healthier parenting in many cases. But, some of those involved in these organizations have mostly seen men as monsters, and maintain a presumption that only fathers are abusive, and that they should be removed from their children's lives as soon as any mother makes any allegation against them – no investigation necessary. Closed case.

For fathers, there are advocates against parental alienation. This is also a good thing, as we have seen that some children do become alienated against one parent, especially in high-conflict divorce. But some of those involved in these organizations have tended mostly to see women as monsters and maintain a presumption that only mothers are alienating parents, and that they should be removed from children's lives as soon as any father makes any allegation against them – no investigation necessary. Closed case.

Fortunately, most parents and most advocates know that both men and women can be abusive, and both men and women can engage in alienating behavior. We have seen many cases involving both men and women as victims and as perpetrators. The solution is in managing the polarity of having two parents and fitting their parenting schedules to the unique circumstances of each child's needs. In other words, each parent has "upsides" and each has "downsides" which need to be balanced without attempting to eliminate one or the other parent. Fortunately, most family courts are starting to take this approach *and* providing protection.

Do today's politics have polarities which can and should be "managed?"

Can We All Get Along?

Democrats and Republicans have some long-standing polarities which have been handled quite well in the past and that have contributed to our national prosperity. All of these polarities can be managed, if we try. Let's consider a few of them:

Individual Freedom vs. Government Regulations: In reality, we need individual freedom and flexibility in where to live, work, play, and so forth. Individuals are generally more creative than organizations, although much of modern technological breakthroughs have included team efforts in research. But, government regulation is also needed, to manage those individuals who take advantage of others, and to coordinate large-scale support for creative individual ventures, and for collective-benefit business ventures – like highways, the Internet, police and fire departments, and the military. We need *both* – individual freedom *and* government regulations. All-or-nothing solutions in these areas have traditionally failed, if people really look at history.

Sexual Freedom/Financial Freedom: Years ago, some wise person pointed out that Democrats have generally promoted personal sexual freedom (including gay marriage and abortion), and Republicans have generally promoted personal financial freedom (including the elimination of taxes and regulations on business). At the same time, each party has promoted government restraints on the other party's preferred domain of personal freedom. Republicans have promoted restraints on abortion and have opposed gay marriage. Democrats have promoted the regulation of business and more taxes on business income. It isn't a question of government regulation or not, it's a question of balance. Personal freedoms are important – and there must be some restraints, as well.

Merit vs. Equality: One of the current political storms in the United States is over the lack of economic mobility for those who work hard. This has been raised as the polarization of the "1%" versus the "99%" of the population. Over the past 30 plus years, liberals and conservatives generally have agreed that most of the nation's economic profit has gone to the wealthiest part of the nation (the top 1%). Should individuals be allowed to gather so much wealth? And, are these the individuals who will create more jobs, if they are free to generate even more wealth with fewer government taxes and regulations?

Is this really an either/or situation? We have always had people who liked to create new products and manage businesses, and who were really good at it. Shouldn't they be rewarded for their hard work? On the other hand, most Americans are hard workers – with an international reputation for not taking much time off. Shouldn't they reap the rewards of a more productive society, as well? This polarity has always been managed in the United States. It's not a question of whether it has been managed, but how.

These are just a sample of the current polarities that are being hotly debated. The question is *how to integrate both poles* of these sorts of issues, rather than *how to eliminate one point of view.*

Can Both Sides have People with Strong Morals?

One of the big splitting dynamics is the tendency to make issues into personal attacks, such as claiming that the other side is evil, insane, incredibly stupid and immoral. Yet, a recent book by Jonathan Haidt compares the way liberals and conservatives think, describing them both as moral – but in different, yet respectable ways. Surprisingly, some of this may be influenced by genetics, as well as by moral traditions.

> Even though the effects of any single gene are tiny, these findings are important because they illustrate one pathway from genes to politics: The genes (collectively) give some people brains that are more (or less) reactive to threats and that produce less (or more) pleasure when exposed to novelty, change, and new experiences. Many studies have shown that conservatives react more strongly than liberals to signs of danger, while novelty-seeking and openness to experience are among the best-established correlates of liberalism.
>
> ....
>
> In my research, I have sought to describe the universal psychological "foundations" of morality. My colleagues at YourMorals.org and I have identified six in particular, six clusters of moral concerns – care/harm, fairness/cheating, liberty/oppression, loyalty/betrayal, authority/subversion, and sanctity/degradation – upon which all political cultures and movements base their moral appeals. Political liberals, we find, tend to rely primarily on care/harm, followed by fairness/cheating and liberty/

> oppression. Social conservatives, in contrast, use all six foundations. They are less concerned than liberals about harm to innocent victims, but they are much more concerned about the moral foundations that bind groups and nations together, i.e., loyalty (patriotism), authority (law and order, traditional families), and sanctity (the Bible, God, the flag) (Haidt, 2012, p. 279).

It's All in the Family Anyway

In 2011, conservative commentator, David Brooks, wrote the following summary of research (Brooks, 2011) about political viewpoints. It was quite surprising (and he was quite non-partisan about reporting it). Rather than analyzing political theories and reading world history, most of us get our political views from closer to home:

> As political scientists Donald Green, Bradley Palmquist, and Eric Schickler argue in their book, PARTISAN HEARTS AND MINDS, most people either inherit their party affiliations from their parents, or they form an attachment to one party or another early in adulthood. Few people switch parties once they hit middle age. Even major historic events such as the world wars and the Watergate scandal do not cause large numbers of people to switch.
>
> Moreover, Green, Palmquist, and Schickler continue, when people do select their own party affiliations, they do not choose parties by comparing platforms and then figuring out where the nation's

> interests lie. Drawing on a vast range of data, the authors argue that party attachment is more like attachment to a religious denomination or a social club. People have stereotypes in their heads about what Democrats are like and what Republicans are like, and they gravitate toward the party made up of people like themselves.
>
> Once they have formed an affiliation, people bend their philosophies and their perceptions of reality so they become more and more aligned with members of their political tribe. Paul Goren of the University of Minnesota has used survey data to track the same voters over time. Under the classic model, you'd expect to find that people who valued equal opportunity would become Democrats and that people who valued limited government would become Republicans. In fact, you're more likely to find that people become Democrats first, then place increasing value on equal opportunity, or they become Republicans first, then place increasing value on limited government. Party affiliation often shapes values, not the other way around (pp. 302-303).

Attack-and-defend cycles just escalate, rather than educate either side.

Ironically, he explains this as having more to do with our "political tribe," than with specific positions on the issues. Does this sound familiar? When high-conflict politicians are involved, this sets up a high risk for tribal warfare, just as we see in high-conflict divorce. When positions are driven by personal attacks, crisis emotions, and all-or-nothing thinking, it's not surprising that it results in strengthened allegiance to one's political tribe, either for one side or the other. And, the more they do this, the easier they can resolve whatever cognitive dissonance remains in their thoughts. Attack-and-defend cycles just escalate, rather than educate either side. That's been the experience of family courts over the past decade, and now it looks like the trend in politics.

Can we get out of this cycle? Unfortunately, the people in power who are most concerned about this process are leaving. And those we would most want to discourage are running hard to "take back" the country from one side or the other.

What Can Be Done?

We both are family mediators. We have dedicated our careers to the resolution of relationship conflict in some of the most challenging areas of human relations. We have recommendations for three groups of people:

A. For politicians

You can defend yourself without personal attacks against your opponent. Two methods can accomplish this:

1. Use E.A.R. Statements (*Empathy, Attention, Respect)* – when someone attacks you in person:
Try to connect with the person by making a statement that shows *Empathy, Attention* and *Respect*

for the person. While this is the opposite of what you feel like doing, it will actually gain you respect (especially if people see you do this in public) and calm down the person criticizing you. For example: "I can see how strongly you feel about this issue (Empathy). I want to pay attention to your concerns (Attention). I have a lot of respect for your efforts to explain the problem and your suggested solutions (Respect)."

This usually reduces the tension in the room or gathering and shows that you are able to treat everyone with respect, even those who disagree strongly with you. Of course, your tone of voice needs to be sincere, rather than showing disdain, as you may be tempted to do. If you can succeed at this, you will be amazed at how much respect you will earn in other people's eyes. We have taught this method to thousands of people and the feedback is very positive.

2. Use B.I.F.F. Responses (*Brief, Informative, Friendly* and *Firm*) – when someone writes something attacking you:

Respond with a message that is Brief, Informative, Friendly, and Firm. This is another method taught to thousands of parents, legal professionals and managers dealing with high-conflict people (Eddy, 2011). This method doesn't take long at all. Here's an example, in response to a personal attack claiming that you are a naïve or irresponsible politician:

"I appreciate hearing your opinions on this important issue facing our country. I have been studying this problem and many of the solutions that have been tried in the past. I know that some people would like me to take this action of ________________________, as you suggest. However, that approach has unfortunately failed and made matters worse in the past. I can give you several examples, such as: __________________
__________________________.

I am seeking the best advice I can obtain from a wide number of experts and everyday people. I welcome the concerns of my opponent in this election and appreciate this chance to respond. These are not easy problems and we will need everyone's help to successfully manage them."

B. For individuals

We encourage you to learn and practice the above two methods, which can be very helpful in everyday life whenever you are personally attacked, either in person or in writing. If you are dealing with a political discussion, these are particularly helpful methods, as they can calm the discussion and earn you respect.

During elections, we also recommend that you look at the patterns of each candidate's long-term behavior. Notice that some people are naturally "high-conflict" in their behavior, while others may reluctantly par-

ticipate in it out of self-defense. In particular, note the following:

1. Watch out for personal attacks. "Separate the person from the problem." This insight has been around at least since Harvard negotiation professors William Ury and Roger Fisher published their landmark book, *Getting to Yes,* in 1983. In fact, this was their number one message to learn for managing any successful negotiation – whether negotiating about buying a car or ending a war. Calling the other person unfit to lead, or a job-killer, or what-have-you, is not designed to educate you about the issues. It's designed to make you angry and reactive. Don't fall for it. Ask questions about their policies and proposals. And, don't forget to ask yourself: *Is this really a crisis? Is this really a hero?*

2. Don't get emotionally hooked by inappropriate crisis emotions. These emotional alarms heighten personal attacks. You can hear the politician's voice rise, as he (or she) blames lots of current problems on the other candidate. This emotional rise in tone of voice unconsciously triggers your amygdala and shuts down your logical, problem-solving thinking. Next thing you know, you are feeling really angry or disgusted at the target of blame you just heard about. Remember, this emotional amygdala alarm can be set off unconsciously – without you even realizing it. Political attack ad consultants have spent a lifetime and millions of dollars in researching how to do this. Always ask yourself: *Is this really a crisis? Is this person really a hero?*

3. **Beware of all-or-nothing solutions.** They may sound great on the surface and have some needed truth in them. But they are often only one part of the puzzle. As the Polarity Management researchers tell us, if you don't consider other points of view, you risk getting deeply into the downside of your own perspective. Look for the whole picture, which includes upsides and downsides of both points of view.

4. **Recognize the signs of narcissistic behavior.** High-conflict politicians with lots of narcissism are often the best at fooling voters, until they are in office. They are *self-absorbed, lack empathy* for others, and *misjudge others* – they are blind to the realities of how other people might think in a conflict. They see peace and turn it into war, envisioning enemies everywhere. They are preoccupied with *seeing themselves as heroes* (because they see enemies everywhere), yet they make decisions and take actions which show that they are quite the opposite. For these reasons, they *don't play well with others.* Negotiation and compromise are dirty words for them in relationships. Unfortunately, these traits usually only come to the surface after they have done their damage. See if you can catch these warning signs beforehand.

5. **Turn off the blaming messages of each candidate's negative advocates.** Repetition is the most powerful way that high-conflict people get you to vote for them. With today's news media, you can hear certain messages literally hundreds of times. Attack ads work, because you hear the exact same words and tone of voice, until your mind has memorized it – without

even thinking about it! Super PACs know this works, and we have given several examples. All that's needed is enough money to play ads over and over again on TV and in other news media. Remember Newt Gingrich and his "baggage?" Remember "Obamacare?" These terms are designed to manipulate you quickly and are out of reach of your logical thinking. Turn them off when they come on, if you can.

C. **For society at large**

1. **Set limits on high-conflict election behavior.** High-conflict people (including politicians) are mostly unable to stop themselves, so it is necessary to have social rules and consequences to limit their damage to society. Narcissists hate rules, but they need them more than everyone else. They can't stop themselves. Encourage your representatives to pass laws that will set limits on the extreme behavior that recent decisions have allowed.

2. **Support efforts to pass campaign disclosure laws** requiring the disclosure of campaign contributions and limitations on the amount that any one person or group (corporation, union, etc.) can donate to a campaign. This should also include any group working to assist or criticize a candidate from outside the campaign, such as Super PACs. Massive amounts of money significantly distort and potentially will destroy our participatory democracy. Remember that the McCain-Feingold law (promoted jointly by a Republican and a Democrat) was unable to control outside groups. We can't let this continue.

Conclusion

For over 30 years, we each have been dealing with children and families going through divorce – as a psychologist, and as an attorney, and both of us as family mediators. Over this time, we have observed the increase in the number and percentages of divorces that are high-conflict. There are many causes, but we have especially noted an increase in the following:

- The over-emphasis on high-conflict behavior in general on TV, in movies, and on the Internet.
- An excess of narcissism (self-centeredness and uncaring) in society at large.
- The role-modeling of high-conflict behavior among our nation's leaders.
- High-conflict behavior among some divorce professionals and other negative advocates that are very adversarial.

These have resulted in more parents who cannot talk with each other or share parenting, and in more children who grow up resisting or hating a parent. The cost to society is huge, as millions of dollars are spent each year on these high-conflict divorces, and the tension in families ripples to relatives and friends.

Professionals increasingly are refusing to take family court cases into their practices, in order to avoid these high-conflict families and focus more on those families with members who can work together. Yet, those who need help the most are getting it the least, and they are left staying in high-conflict. Many of these divorce conflicts last for years longer than the marriages and don't end until one side runs out of money, or just gives up, or runs away.

We have learned some of the warning signs of high-conflict divorces. There is a pattern of behavior, which may be obvious from the start, or may show up by surprise in the middle of the case:

- **Personal attacks** (calling the other person crazy, stupid, immoral or evil).

- **Crisis emotions** (dramatic speech which triggers fear and hatred).

- **All-or-nothing solutions** (eliminate Dad or Mom, take all the assets, take full custody of the children, etc.).

- **Narcissistic behavior** (self-centered, lacks empathy, sees self as big hero).

- **Presence of negative advocates** (who join a side in the hostility).

This seems to be the same pattern we are seeing in today's high-conflict elections. These high-conflict behaviors may be part of the personality of a politician – who we would call a high-conflict politician and would predict future disasters associated with them.

Others simply mirror this high-conflict behavior out of fear or pressure from advisors, but it's not really part of their personality.

Yet, they are still a problem, because their "adopted" high-conflict behavior can spill over into future decisions and behavior, which still may be harmful to the rest of us.

We also see these negative high-conflict behaviors being amplified by Super PACs that fund attack ads in the media; these are organizations of people who are well-paid to repeat the message over and over again. They are negative advocates for the high-conflict politicians, just as some well-paid professionals become negative advocates in high-conflict divorce.

Unfortunately, this is not a game! Voters suffer, and the nation suffers because of it – just as painfully as children suffer in high-conflict divorce.

The Future

The answer seems to lie primarily in learning how to accept and balance the polarities of modern political viewpoints. While the research shows that this has been done adequately for years, it is failing now because of a lack of self-restraint and public restraint. Just as our nation has learned that cigarettes should not be advertised on TV, we need regulations protecting the public from political attack ads that are harmful to us, whether they are the scary Willie Horton type, or the slickly produced type that pretend to be friendly. These methods, that are out of control, are harmful to the health and future of our nation.

Last, we each can increase our own awareness and our own self-restraint. We can turn off politicians who play the high-conflict splitting game, and reward those who don't. We can collaborate with each other to solve problems and manage polarities, and we can mediate our differences when necessary.

We are, after all, the American Family. It's up to us! Let's encourage and choose leaders who can treat us all with empathy and respect.

Best Wishes!

High-Conflict Politician Scorecard

As we have explained in this book, high-conflict politicians have won elections and then turned into huge mistakes – either getting thrown out of office for their misdeeds or making high-conflict decisions that have cost our nation dearly. In order to help you notice the warning signs, we have come up with a short checklist to consider for potential candidates:

On-going Traits	**Regular pattern of behavior**								
	None	Mild		Moderate		Often		Very Often	
Personal Attacks	0	1	2	3	4	5	6	7	8
Crisis Emotions	0	1	2	3	4	5	6	7	8
All-or-nothing solutions	0	1	2	3	4	5	6	7	8
Self-absorbed	0	1	2	3	4	5	6	7	8
Lacks empathy	0	1	2	3	4	5	6	7	8
Misjudges others	0	1	2	3	4	5	6	7	8
Sees self as big hero	0	1	2	3	4	5	6	7	8
Doesn't play well with others	0	1	2	3	4	5	6	7	8
TOTAL SCORE = __________									

This "scorecard" is proposed as a guide for comparing candidates, and not a research-based formula. To a great extent, high-conflict behavior is in the eye of the beholder. There is no cut-off or clear line between "reasonable" people and "high-conflict" people. It is possible that some elections are between two candidates who both score high or both score low on this list, while other elections may present more clear-cut situations, with one low and one high. Simply thinking about these behaviors should help you become less vulnerable to attack ads and other manipulations by high-conflict politicians in federal, state and local elections.

Acknowledgements

The development of this book represents our effort at a low-conflict, creative collaboration. In working together efficiently, we developed this concept, did our research, drafted chapters, melded them together, received input from numerous readers (colleagues, friends and family members – including Democrats and Republicans), and – after many lively discussions and numerous compromises – submitted it for publication. We couldn't have done this alone and really appreciate each other's like-minded thinking and writing on this subject.

We are deeply grateful to our wonderfully supportive publisher, Megan Hunter, the CEO of HCI Press, who fully understands high-conflict behavior and the destructive effects it can have. With an awesome sense of humor and her capable capacity to multi-task, Megan managed miracles in getting this book out in its timely fashion; if only Congress could be so effective!

We also want to thank our creative book designer, Elle Phillips, especially for coming up with the cover design that exquisitely captures the very essence of our book. And Kim Clougherty deserves extra credit for all of her work finalizing the page-by-page layout and giving it that extra special touch.

To our friends, family, and colleagues who, over the years, have contributed to our ideas about conflict, divorce, and politics, we extend special appreciation. You know who you are!

And, most of all, to our respective, and respected wives, Alice (Bill's wife) and Donna (Don's wife), we thank you both for your faithful support through those inevitable late night hours of writing and editing, and for your perceptive contributions regarding political and family cultures.

References

Ahrons, C. R. (1994). *The Good Divorce: Keeping Your Family Together When Your Marriage Comes Apart.* New York: Harper Collins.

Ahrons, C. R. (2004). *We're Still Family: What Grown Children Have to Say about Their Parents' Divorce.* New York: HarperCollins.

Auletta, K. (2010). Non-Stop News: With Cable, the Web, and Tweets, Can the President – or the Press – Still Control the Story? *The New Yorker.* Jan. 25, 2010.

Bai, M. (2012, July 21). How Much Has Citizens United Changed the Political Game? *The New York Times.* Politics.

Baldwin, A. (2008). *A Promise to Ourselves.* New York: St. Martin's Press.

_____ (2012, July 14). *The Boston Globe.* The Associated Press.

Brooks, D. (2011). *The Social Animal: The Hidden Sources of Love, Character, and Achievement.* New York: Random House.

Brownstone, H. (2009). *Tug of War: A Judge's Verdict on Separation, Custody Battles, and the Bitter Realities of Family Court.* Toronto, Ontario: ECW Press.

Bush, G. W. (2010). *Decision Points*. New York: The Crown Publishing Group.

Cloud, J. (2009, January 8). The Mystery of Borderline Personality Disorder. *Time*. January 8, 2009.

Eddy, B. (2011). *BIFF: Quick Responses to High Conflict People, Their Personal Attacks, Hostile Email and Social Media Meltdowns*. Scottsdale, AZ: HCI Press.

Eddy, B. (2006, 2008). *High Conflict People in Legal Disputes*. Scottsdale, AZ: HCI Press.

Eddy, B. and Kreger, R. (2011). *Splitting: Protecting Yourself While Divorcing Someone with Borderline or Narcissistic Personality Disorder*. Oakland, CA: New Harbinger Press.

Friedman, E. (2008, August 12). Politicians' Biggest Battle: Themselves. ABC News.com. Health.

Goleman, D. (2006). *Social Intelligence: The New Science of Human Relationships*. New York: Bantam Dell, A Division of Random House.

Gottman, J. (1994). *Why Marriages Succeed or Fail: And How You Can Make Yours Last*. New York: Simon & Schuster Paperbacks.

Haidt, J. (2012). *The Righteous Mind*. New York: Pantheon Books.

Iacoboni, L. (2008). *Mirroring People: The New Science of How We Connect With Others*. New York: Farrar, Straus and Giroux.

Johnson, B. (1992; 1996). *Polarity Management: Identifying and Managing Unsolvable Problems.* Amherst, Massachusetts: HRD Press.

Johnston, J.R. and Campbell, L.E.G. (1988). *Impasses of Divorce: The Dynamics and Resolution of Family Conflict.* New York: The Free Press.

Kelly, J. and Johnston, J.R. (2001). The Alienated Child: A Reformulation of Parental Alienation Syndrome. *Family Court Review, 39* (3), 249-266.

Matthews, D. (2011). Everything you need to know about the Fairness Doctrine in one post. *Ezra Klein's Wonkblog, The Washington Post.* Posted August 23, 2011. http://www.washingtonpost.com/blogs/ezra-klein/post/everything-you-need-to-know-about-the-fairness-doctrine-in-one-post/2011/08/23/gIQAN8CXZJ_blog.html

Mayer, J. (2012). Attack Dog: The Creator of the Willie Horton Ad Is Going All Out for Mitt Romney. *The New Yorker*, February 13, 2012.

Millon, T. (1996). *Disorders of Personality: DSM-IV and Beyond.* New York: John Wiley & Sons.

Navaro, J. (2005). *Hunting Terrorists: A Look at the Psychopathology of Terror.* Springfield, IL: Charles C. Thomas Publisher, Ltd.

Packer, G. (2010, August 9). The Empty Chamber: Just How Broken Is the Senate? *The New Yorker.* August 9, 2010.

Rutenberg, J. (2004, August 6). Anti-Kerry Ad Is Condemned By McCain. *New York Times.*

Saposnek, D.T. (1983). *Mediating Child Custody Disputes: A Systematic Guide for Family therapists, Court Counselors, Attorneys, and Judges.* San Francisco: Jossey-Bass.

Saposnek, D.T. (1998). *Mediating Child Custody Disputes: A Strategic Approach.* San Francisco: Jossey-Bass/Wiley.

Schore, A. (2012). *The Science of the Art of Psychotherapy.* New York: W.W. Norton & Company.

Svitek, P. (2012, July 6). Pledge Against Taxes Attracts Fewer Republican Candidates. *Huffington Post.* Politics.

Tavris, C. & Aronson, E. (2007). *Mistakes Were Made (But Not by Me): Why We Justify Foolish Beliefs, Bad Decisions, and Hurtful Acts.* Boston: Houghton-Mifflin Harcourt.

Thernstrom, J. (2003). Untying the Knot. *New York Times Magazine,* August 24, 2003, 38-44.

Twenge, J.M. and Campbell, W.K. (2009). *The Narcissism Epidemic: Living in the Age of Entitlement.* New York: The Free Press, a Division of Simon & Schuster, Inc.

William A. ("Bill") Eddy, L.C.S.W., J.D. is a family law attorney, therapist and mediator, with over thirty years experience working with children and families. He is the Senior Family Mediator at the National Conflict Resolution Center in San Diego, California. He is also the President of the High Conflict Institute, which provides speakers, trainers and consultants on the subject of managing high-conflict people in legal disputes, workplace disputes, healthcare and education.

He has taught Negotiation and Mediation at the University of San Diego School of Law and he teaches Psychology of Conflict at the Strauss Institute for Dispute Resolution at Pepperdine University School of Law. He is the author of several books, including:

Splitting: Protecting Yourself While Divorcing Someone with Borderline or Narcissistic Personality Disorder

BIFF: Quick Responses to High Conflict People, Their Personal Attacks, Hostile Email and Social Media Meltdowns

It's All Your Fault! 12 Tips for Managing People Who Blame Others for Everything

His website is: www.HighConflictInstitute.com

Don Saposnek

Donald T. Saposnek, Ph.D. is a clinical-child psychologist, child custody mediator, and family therapist in private practice for over 40 years, and is a national and international trainer of mediation and child development. For the past 35 years, he has been teaching on the psychology faculty at the University of California at Santa Cruz, and is Adjunct Professor at Pepperdine University School of Law's Straus Institute for Dispute Resolution.

He is the author of the classic book, *Mediating Child Custody Disputes,* and has published extensively in the professional literature on child custody and child psychology. He serves on the editorial boards of the *Family Court Review* and *Conflict Resolution Quarterly* journals and is the editor of the international Academy of Professional Family Mediators' *The Professional Family Mediator.*

As director of Family Mediation Service of Santa Cruz, he managed the family court services for 17 years and has mediated nearly 5,000 child custody disputes in both the public and private sectors since 1977.

His website is: www.mediate.com/dsaposnek

Sources for Further Information

For further information on any of the material presented in this book please visit our websites and check out our other publications.

www.hcipress.com

www.HighConflictInstitute.com

www.NewWays4Families.com

www.mediate.com/dsaposnek

Bill Eddy, Don Saposnek and Megan Hunter (CEO at HCI Press) travel the world speaking to groups about these issues and training professionals.

Please feel free to contact them if you are interested in having them speak to your group.

All our books are available in digital format at these retailers:

More books from

BIFF Quick Responses to High Conflict People
by Bill Eddy
ISBN # 978-1-936268-35-1

It's All Your Fault!
by Bill Eddy
ISBN # 978-1-936268-02-3

Don't Alienate the Kids
by Bill Eddy
ISBN # 978-1-936268-03-0

High Conflict People in Legal Disputes
by Bill Eddy
ISBN # 978-1-936268-00-9

Managing High Conflict People in Court
by Bill Eddy
ISBN # 978-1-936268-01-6

The Future of Family Court
by Bill Eddy
ISBN # 978-1-936268-49-8

You can order any of these books from our website
www.hcipress.com
www.unhookedbooks.com

Contact us for bulk pricing

PRESS

CPSIA information can be obtained at www.ICGtesting.com
Printed in the USA
LVOW12s2046090514

385119LV00006B/11/P